COFFEE
CUP
BIBLE
STUDIES

Kona with
Jonah

AMG
PUBLISHERS

SANDRA GLAHN

Coffee Cup Bible Studies
Kona with Jonah

© 2009 by Sandra L. Glahn

Published by AMG Publishers. All Rights Reserved.

Published in association with the MacGregor Literary agency
2373 NW 185th Ave., Suite 165
Hillsboro, OR 97124

First Printing, 2009

ISBN 10: 0-89957-395-9
ISBN 13: 978-089957395-3

Editing and Proofreading: Diane Storz and Rick Steele
Interior Design: PerfecType, Nashville, Tennessee
Cover Design: Bryan Woodlief, Chattanooga, Tennessee

Printed in the United States of America
14 13 12 11 10 09 –L– 6 5 4 3 2 1

For Jonah Wagoner with love

ACKNOWLEDGMENTS

Thank you . . .
- Gary, my love—for partnering with me in every way.
- Dr. Ron (Allen)—for making the prophets of the First Testament come alive.
- Dr. Dorian Coover-Cox—for sharing insights into the Hebrew text that constantly challenge me to consider a more exalted view of God.
- Dr. Jeff Watson and Dr. Bob Chisholm—for working line by line to teach me Jonah as it was written in that funny, backwards, vowels-missing alphabet.
- Members of Biblical Studies Press (bible.org) and translators of the NET Bible—for your help, apart from which the Coffee Cup Bible Studies series would have been impossible. Thank you for working without compensation so others might grow in the Word. May God richly reward you in this life and in the next.
- Dr. Chip MacGregor—for representing me with enthusiasm and good humor, and for consistent prayers.
- Virginia and Karen Swint—for faithful prayers, devoted friendship, and fine editing.
- Cec Murphey—for opening doors for me through wise reinvestment of your earthly blessings.
- Rick Steele and Diane Stortz of AMG—for your expertise in both the biblical text and in editing content.
- Thanks also to my prayer team: Ann Grafe, Willis Grafe, Chris Havlock, Mike Justice, Terri Justice, Ann Knauss, Kelly Knauss,

v

Reiko Kirstein, Jerry Lawrence, Martha McKibben, Beverly Lucas, Barbara Smith, Virginia Swint, Jeni Ward, and Lance Ward. And thanks to all who pray that God will use the Word through this series to change lives. You know who you are, and your contribution is not forgotten. May the Lord reward in public what you have done in secret.

INTRODUCTION TO THE
COFFEE CUP BIBLE STUDY SERIES

The precepts of the LORD are right, rejoicing the heart;
The commandment of the LORD is pure, enlightening the eyes
(Psalm 19:8).

Congratulations! You have chosen wisely. By electing to study the Bible, you are choosing to spend time learning that which will rejoice the heart and enlighten the eyes.

And while any study in the Bible is time well spent, the Coffee Cup Bible Study series has some unique elements. So before we get started, let's consider some of them to help you maximize your study time.

About coffee. You don't have to like coffee to use this series for regular Bible study. Tea works too. So does milk. And water. Or nothing. But embrace the metaphor: take a "coffee break"—a bit of downtime—away from the routine, designed to refresh you. And you can imbibe alone, but you might enjoy the process even more with a group. (More about that coming up.)

Life rhythms. Most participants in Bible studies say they find it easier to keep up on weekdays than on weekends, when the routine changes. Thus, all Coffee Cup Bible Studies contain weekday Bible study questions that require active involvement, but weekend segments consist instead of short readings that kick off and make application of the week's study. Still, the specified days as laid out here serve as mere suggestions. Some prefer to attend a Bible study one day and follow a four-day-per-week study schedule along with weekend readings. Others prefer to take twice as long to get through the book, cutting each day's selection roughly in half. Adapt the structure of days to fit your own needs.

Community. While you can complete this study individually, consider going through it with a few others. If you don't already belong to a Bible study group, find some friends and start one, or connect periodically with others who organize short-term online groups announced at www.soulpersuit.com. These vehicles give you opportunities to share what you're learning with a wider community and gain from their insights too.

Aesthetics. At the author's Web site (www.aspire2.com) in a section designed for the Coffee Cup series, you will find links to art that relates to each Bible study. For *Kona with Jonah* you'll discover works such as Gustave Doré's "Jonah Preaching to the Ninevites," for example. (You'll also find links to other studies in Jonah, good commentaries, and resource material.) The more senses you can engage in your interaction with God's truth, the more you'll enjoy it and remember it.

Convenience. Rather than turning in your Bible to find the passages for study, you'll find the entire text for each day included in this Coffee Cup Bible Studies book. While it's important to know our way around the Bible, the series is designed so you can stash your book in a purse, diaper bag, briefcase, or backpack and have everything you need, making it easy to use on the subway, at a coffee shop, in a doctor's waiting room, or on your lunch break.

Why does the Coffee Cup series use the *NET Bible* translation? Accessible online from anywhere in the world, the *NET* (New English Translation) *Bible* is a modern translation from the ancient Greek, Hebrew, and Aramaic texts. A team of biblical-language scholars volunteered their time to prepare it because they shared a vision to make the Bible available worldwide without the high cost of permissions usually required for using copyrighted materials. Any other translation, with the exception of the *King James Version,* would have made the cost of including the text here prohibitive. Only through the generosity of the Biblical Studies Press and the *NET Bible* translators is this convenience possible. (For more information on this ministry, go to www.bible.org.)

Sensitivity to time and culture considerations. Many Bible studies begin by guiding readers to observe and interpret the words written to the original audience (the exegetical step) and then apply the words directly to a contemporary setting (the homiletical step). They skip what we would call the theological step. The result is sometimes misapplication. For example, Paul told slaves to obey their *masters,* and many studies might conclude, that we need to obey our *employers.* Yet today's bosses don't own their employees, nor do they usually share the same household. Employment is by mutual agreement; slavery is not, so we should probably use the voluntary *submit* rather than the obligatory *obey* when referring to an employment context. In the Coffee Cup series, our aim is to be particularly sensitive to the audience to whom the "mail" was addressed, but also to take the crucial step of separating what was intended for a limited audience from that which is for all audiences for all time (in the example of slaves and masters, respect for those in authority).

Sensitivity to genre. Rather than crafting a series in which each study is laid out exactly like all the others, each Coffee Cup study is structured to best present the genre category examined—whether epistle (letter), poetry, gospel, history, or narrative. The way we study a story (narrative) such as Jonah differs from how someone might study the compact poetry in Song of Songs or an epistle such as Philippians. So while the studies in the Coffee Cup series may have similar elements, each study takes the approach to the text that best fits the genre. Whereas a study in Philippians will include numerous word studies, for example, a narrative such as Jonah will focus on fewer exact terms and more on story elements, such as irony or contrast.

Selections for memorization. A Cuban pastor incarcerated in deplorable conditions for his faith afterward told my friend, "The Word of God was of great comfort. One Methodist pastor took a notebook and a pencil and wrote down all the Scriptures that everyone knew by heart and recorded them for all of us to read the Word of God." In the absence of Bibles, the only access these prisoners had to God's Word was what they'd hidden in their hearts—treasure their captors could never take away. Whether we live where Christians endure persecution or we're tempted by apathy from materialism's pull, we need God's Word in our hearts to help us stand strong in every situation. So each week you'll find a verse or two to memorize.

Are you ready? Fasten your seat belt and fly back in time to the ancient Near East, where our journey begins.

INTRODUCTION TO
KONA WITH JONAH

"Pray for our troops in Iraq." How often during turbulent times have these words echoed through churches and across e-waves? Yet when did we also hear "Pray for al Qaeda"?

Are you kidding? They behead people—good people. People seeking peace. People who have sacrificed physical comfort to care for others who are oppressed. If al Qaeda is mentioned in our prayers at all, it's because we're asking God to "do lightning."

In the Book of Jonah, readers encounter God's love for the murderous enemies of Israel. The particular objects of the Lord's grace in this case are the people of Nineveh—located near modern-day Mosul, Iraq. In Jonah's encounter with those who are so loathsome to him, readers come face-to-face with a God whose mercy stands in contrast with humanity's propensity to hate.

To set the scene for exploring Jonah, we need to know some essentials.

Time. The events in the Book of Jonah take place in a capital in the Middle East about three hundred years before Esther serves as Persia's queen. That sets it somewhere around 793–753 BC—before the northern and southern divisions of Israel are dragged off into exile.

Author. The text says nothing about who wrote the Book of Jonah or when. On the one hand, it might seem unlikely that Jonah himself wrote it, as he doesn't come off looking so great. On the other hand, he would have been the person most familiar with the circumstances and the only one who knew what he prayed in the fish's belly. If indeed Jonah wrote the book, we can read between the lines and assume he had a major change of heart after his close encounters with God—a possibility that should give hope to those of us who struggle with forgiveness.

Jonah the man. Every writing prophet in the Bible has God's name as part of his own—except Jonah. Instead of having a moniker like "God will uplift" (Jeremiah) or "Salvation of Yahweh" (Isaiah), Jonah has a name that means "silly dove." *Hmm.* Is that supposed to provide us a hint about his character? Through Jonah's story we do indeed see a picture of a silly, flighty little bird who can't seem to fly the right direction without help. Jonah is the only negatively portrayed prophet in the Bible, and the only one who travels to speak to a country other than his own. According to 2 Kings 14:25, Jonah was the son of Amittai of Gath Hepher. He lived and labored either in the early part of Jeroboam II's reign or during the preceding generation. This same passage tells us that Jonah predicted the restoration of the land of Israel to its ancient boundaries through the efforts of

Hollywood Tie-Ins

Jonah: A Great Fish Story (2005). In this cartoon adaptation of the well-known story, stop-motion animation and computer graphics convey a lesson on obedience and faith.

Jonah: A Veggie Tales Movie (2002). This VeggieTales film features Bob the Tomato and the Veggie kids learning the story of Jonah. God charges the prophet with the task of delivering a message to the people of Nineveh, but he ends up in the belly of a fish.

Moby Dick (1956). Gregory Peck stars as the obsessed Captain Ahab in this big-screen version of Herman Melville's classic novel. John Huston directed this faithful adaptation, which racked up numerous critics' awards. Moby Dick is not the story of Jonah per se, but it contains many literary allusions to the biblical Jonah.

Moby Dick (1998). Herman Melville's classic book gets a makeover in this TV miniseries. Ishmael (Henry Thomas) tells the story of Captain Ahab (Patrick Stewart), the man obsessed with catching the white whale. Gregory Peck won a supporting actor Golden Globe for his final role as Father Mapple. The series also received Emmy nominations for best miniseries, best actor (Stewart), and best supporting actor (Peck).

Jeroboam II. The village of Gath Hepher was located in the territory of Zebulun (Josh. 19:13)[1] on the coast.

Theme. The Book of Jonah is a satire, probably designed to make its original audience—the nation of Israel— knowingly laugh their way to the final line. Its theme is God's broad mercy in contrast with humanity's self-indulgence. This theme falls within the larger theme of the Bible's prophetic books, which is that in wrath God will remember mercy. Also like the other prophetic books, the Book of Jonah reminds its intended audience that announcements of judgment are nearly always opportunities to receive grace.

Main idea. The main idea in Jonah is that God desires to show mercy to *all* people—even scourge-of-the-earth (in the minds of the Israelites) Assyrians.

Back story. To understand what was happening to Jonah and his people at the time the story takes place, it's important to review a brief history of Israel.

Thousands of years prior to our story, Abram, though childless, received a promise from God that he would become a great nation (see Gen. 12). And God kept his promise. Isaac, conceived in Abraham and Sarah's old age, was the son of promise. Isaac had a son named Jacob, later also referred to as Israel. Jacob had twelve sons and a daughter, and one of those sons was Joseph—the favorite son to whom Jacob gave a coat of many colors. (See *Joseph: King of Dreams* or *Joseph and the Amazing Technicolor Dreamcoat*, or, of course, read the second half of Genesis.)

Joseph's jealous brothers sold him to slavery in Egypt, and decades later those same brothers came begging at his door during a terrible famine. By that time Joseph had risen from slavery to power, and he—through God's sovereignty—saved the brothers from starvation. So Joseph's kin settled in Egypt and multiplied over a period of about 470 years.

Sadly, during these centuries Abraham's descendants eventually fell from power and ended up as slaves. When they cried out to God, the Lord sent Moses to lead them from bondage back to their promised land. (Watch *The Ten Commandments*, *The Prince of Egypt*, or, of course, read the book of Exodus.)

Back in their homeland, the twelve tribes of Israel were ruled by judges—rather than monarchs—appointed by God. (As He Himself

---

[1] International Standard Bible Encyclopedia, CD-ROM, "Jonah."

was their king, God preferred judges to human kings; see the Book of Judges). Yet the people insisted on having a king like the other nations around them, so eventually God let them have their way (read 1 and 2 Kings and 1 and 2 Chronicles).

At first the twelve tribes were united under the reigns of Kings Saul, David, and Solomon (read 1 and 2 Samuel). Yet eventually the nation split, with ten tribes making up the northern kingdom, Israel, and two tribes constituting the southern kingdom, Judah. At that point Israel and Judah crowned their own kings.

During this dual-nation period eight centuries before Christ, Jonah lived in the northern kingdom—the capital of which was Samaria. (Sometimes the entire northern kingdom was called Samaria as well.) The prophet's Israelite audience would have included the unredeemed, the wayward, and a handful of the devoted in this section of the divided kingdom. Perhaps the people made up an unimpressive group spiritually speaking, but at least (in Jonah's mind) they weren't *barbaric* like their enemies.

The Israelite king in power during Jonah's life expanded his territory, so in terms of economics, times were good. But the biblical author of 2 Kings describes this ruler as doing "evil in the sight of the Lord" (2 Kings 14:24). The people had half-hearted faith, and everybody knew their prosperity was short-lived. The mighty Assyrians, named for Ashur (or Assur), their warrior god, were a nearby, powerful Semitic people, and they had threatened to invade, impale, behead, dismember, and display the Israelites.

Nineveh lay at the heart of the Assyrian empire. Classical writers tell us the trapezoid-shaped city was the New York of its time and had a reputation as the world's most barbarous city. Think genocide. Rather than taking war prisoners, Assyria massacred enemy soldiers. They also beheaded opposing kings and hung their heads from trees. Then they exiled conquered members of the upper class, leaving the powerless in burned-out, heavily taxed cities. The mere mention of Assyria evoked fear.

At a time when these evil people threatened his nation, Jonah received a word from God: "Go to Nineveh. Cry against them."

Now, Jonah knew God well enough to know what that meant. Yes, God wanted Jonah to speak words of judgment. But Jonah knew that behind such an assignment was God's mercy, because if God wanted to destroy Nineveh, he would have judged without warning. Any time God *announces* judgment, he's likely giving people a chance

An Assyrian Warrior

to repent. And the last assignment Jonah wanted was to give his enemies such an opportunity. The way he saw it, the wicked terrorist Assyrians might just fear God for a season and wiggle out of judgment when they really deserved to fry. Jonah's own king did evil in God's sight. What if the Ninevites repented and his own king didn't?

It was just like God to give the ferocious Assyrians a warning, because the Lord is full of lovingkindness, slow to anger, and has a heart for all to worship in truth—even if they have the character of death-row inmates. Jonah knew this, and it annoyed him to no end.

This study explores Jonah's story. In it we learn much more than a chronology about an Israelite prophet. We also catch a glimpse of

God's heart for the lost and the compassion of heaven for a nation of hopeless causes. More than that, we also discover the response God wants his followers to have toward all people, even the most flagrantly violent and immoral, including their enemies. *Especially* their enemies.

CONTENTS

WEEK 1 OF 4

Run for Your Life: Jonah 1:1–7

SUNDAY: GET THE WHOLE PICTURE

Scripture: He prayed to the LORD and said, "Oh, LORD, this is just what I thought would happen when I was in my own country. This is what I tried to prevent by attempting to escape to Tarshish!—because I knew that you are gracious and compassionate, slow to anger and abounding in mercy, and one who relents concerning threatened judgment" (Jon. 4:2).

Have you ever felt God can't be trusted? Maybe you haven't, but I sure have. Back when I was in college, I had thoughts like, I'm afraid to fully give my life to God because he'd probably make me go to *Africa.*

Looking back, I have no idea what I was so afraid of. I went to Africa last summer and loved it.

Here's the thing: If we read only the first chapter of the Book of Jonah, we might conclude that God always makes his followers do the opposite of what they want. Jonah's book opens with a word from the Lord to the prophet, directing him to go to his enemies and warn them of impending judgment. Jonah hated Iraqis, so he ran the other direction. Instead of traveling east over land to the capital of Assyria, he high-tailed it west to Joppa for a ride on the high sea. After Jonah boarded the boat, though, a tempest tossed the vessel, and Jonah got thrown overboard. Next thing he knew, he was soaking in the stomach acid of a giant fish.

Does God sound nice to you in that story?

Yet the first chapter of Jonah is not the whole story, is it? Which is precisely my point.

If we draw conclusions from reading only one chapter instead of the entire book, we risk making all sorts of incorrect assumptions about God's character. Why? Because we haven't read the entire account, and the main point in a story emerges only after we get the whole picture.

Jonah is a narrative. And a danger in studying a Bible story only one chapter per week is that we see just part of the whole with each reading. That's why we'll begin our study by reading the entire Book of Jonah—so we can grasp its overall message. *Then* we'll break it down by chapters, always looking for how the smaller snapshots fit into the bigger picture.

So bear in mind this principle for studying Bible stories: *consider the entire narrative to find the message the author intended.*

Have you ever watched *The Sound of Music*? Imagine if all you saw of the movie included a nun-to-be caring for some ornery kids and falling in love with their father; then that father brings home a gorgeous, rich woman and announces his engagement. If you saw only this much of the show, what might you conclude is its message—men are attracted only to rich, beautiful women? God will punish a nun-to-be who falls in love with anyone but him? You could come up with any number of whacked-out ideas that would have nothing whatsoever to do with the actual plot.

And the same is true of the Book of Jonah. If we read chapter 1 and see only a man running away and suffering for his disobedience, we find ourselves pretty far off course from what the original author had in mind.

So what *should* we conclude from Jonah's story? Once we've read the entire book, we see that the story focuses on God's compassion:

- God cares deeply about the lost.
- God is omnipresent. No one can ever really run or hide from the Almighty.
- God is in control.
- God bestows favor on some, not so they can merely soak up blessing but so they can share the good news with others.
- Sometimes God's own people demonstrate less compassion toward the lost than the lost show to God's people.
- Words of impending judgment are really a merciful, last-chance opportunity to repent.
- God wants us to obey *and* to trust.

Finally, the main idea of the entire book is this: the LORD is "gracious and compassionate, slow to anger and abounding in mercy, and one who relents concerning threatened judgment" (Jon. 4:2). We see this illustrated through God's compassion in sending Jonah to his evil enemies. God chose the nation of Israel as His people, but not so they could sit around sunning themselves in grace and enjoying privileged status as the Sovereign One's pet. Through the shining light of Israel, the Almighty wanted people from every tribe and nation to receive the offer of grace.

All of the truths from the Book of Jonah are still true today. God cares for the lost. The Almighty is everywhere. The sovereign one is in control. The Lord wants to use those blessed with divine favor to spread the good news. The king wants us to have compassion on our enemies—because we ourselves have received compassion. God is good. And we must trust.

I alluded earlier to the trip my family and I took to Africa last summer. There we met Christ-followers who joyfully live on less money in a year than we blow through in a week. And whereas sometimes we use prayer as a last resort, they think of it as their first line of defense. I learned much from my African brothers and sisters. And now, ironically, I find myself hoping that maybe God will send us to Africa again.

What are you afraid the Lord will do to you if you follow completely? Will you trust God's heart?

1. The Book of Jonah is about the length of a short magazine article. Pray for God to grant you insight; then read the entire Book of Jonah in one sitting. Focus on identifying the prophet's attitudes.

Jonah 1

1:1 The LORD said to Jonah son of Amittai, **1:2** "Go immediately to Nineveh, that large capital city, and announce judgment against its people because their wickedness has come to my attention." **1:3** Instead, Jonah immediately headed off to Tarshish to escape from the commission of the LORD. He traveled to Joppa and found a merchant ship heading to Tarshish. So he paid the fare and went aboard it to go with them to Tarshish far away from the LORD. **1:4** But the LORD hurled a powerful wind on the sea. Such a violent tempest arose on the sea that the ship threatened to break up! **1:5** The sailors were so afraid that each cried out to his own god and they flung the ship's cargo overboard to make the ship lighter. Jonah, meanwhile, had gone down into the hold below deck, had lain down, and was sound asleep. **1:6** The ship's captain approached him and said, "What are you doing asleep? Get up! Cry out to your god! Perhaps your god might take notice of us so that we might not die!" **1:7** The sailors said to one another, "Come on, let's cast lots to find out whose fault it is that this disaster has overtaken us." So they cast lots, and Jonah was singled out. **1:8** They said to him, "Tell us, whose fault is it that this disaster has overtaken us? What's your occupation? Where do you come from? What's your country? And who are your people?" **1:9** He said to them, "I am a Hebrew! And I worship the LORD, the God of heaven, who made the sea and the dry land." **1:10** Hearing this, the men became even more afraid and said to him, "What have you done?" (The men said this because they knew that he was trying to escape from the LORD, because he had previously told them.) **1:11** Because the storm was growing worse and worse, they said to him, "What should we do to you to make the sea calm down for us?" **1:12** He said to them, "Pick me up and throw me into the sea to make the sea quiet down, because I know it's my fault you are in this severe storm." **1:13** Instead, they tried to row back to land, but they were not able to do so because the storm kept growing worse and worse. **1:14** So they cried out to the LORD, "Oh, please, LORD, don't let us die on account of this man! Don't hold us guilty of shedding innocent blood. After all, you, LORD, have done just as you pleased." **1:15** So they picked Jonah up and threw him into the sea, and the sea stopped raging. **1:16** The men feared the LORD greatly, and earnestly vowed to offer lavish sacrifices to the LORD.

1:17 The LORD sent a huge fish to swallow Jonah, and Jonah was in the stomach of the fish three days and three nights.

Jonah 2

2:1 Jonah prayed to the LORD his God from the stomach of the fish

2:2 and said, "I called out to the LORD from my distress,

and he answered me;

from the belly of Sheol I cried out for help,

and you heard my prayer.

2:3 You threw me into the deep waters,

into the middle of the sea;

the ocean current engulfed me;

all the mighty waves you sent swept over me.

2:4 I thought I had been banished from your sight,

that I would never again see your holy temple!

2:5 Water engulfed me up to my neck;

the deep ocean surrounded me;

seaweed was wrapped around my head.

2:6 I went down to the very bottoms of the mountains;

the gates of the netherworld barred me in forever;

but you brought me up from the Pit, O LORD, my God.

2:7 When my life was ebbing away, I called out to the LORD,

and my prayer came to your holy temple.

2:8 Those who worship worthless idols forfeit the mercy that could be theirs.

2:9 But as for me, I promise to offer a sacrifice to you with a public declaration of praise;

I will surely do what I have promised.

Salvation belongs to the LORD!"

2:10 Then the LORD commanded the fish and it disgorged Jonah on dry land.

Jonah 3

3:1 The LORD said to Jonah a second time, **3:2** "Go immediately to Nineveh, that large city, and proclaim to it the message that I tell you." **3:3** So Jonah went immediately to Nineveh, as the LORD had said. (Now Nineveh was an enormous city—it required three days to walk through it!) **3:4** When Jonah began to enter the city one day's walk, he announced, "At the end of forty days, Nineveh will be overthrown!"

3:5 The people of Nineveh believed in God, and they declared a fast and put on sackcloth, from the greatest to the least of them. **3:6** When the news reached the king of Nineveh, he got up from his throne, took off his royal robe, put on sackcloth, and sat on ashes. **3:7** He issued a proclamation and said, "In Nineveh, by the decree of the king and his nobles: No human or animal, cattle or sheep, is to taste anything; they must not eat and they must not drink water. **3:8** Every person and animal must put on sackcloth and must cry earnestly to God, and everyone must turn from their evil way of living and from the violence that they do. **3:9** Who knows? Perhaps God might be willing to change his mind and relent and turn from his fierce anger so that we might not die." **3:10** When God saw their actions—they turned from their evil way of living!—God relented concerning the judgment he had threatened them with and he did not destroy them.

Jonah 4

4:1 This displeased Jonah terribly and he became very angry. **4:2** He prayed to the LORD and said, "Oh, LORD, this is just what I thought would happen when I was in my own country. This is what I tried to prevent by attempting to escape to Tarshish!—because I knew that you are gracious and compassionate, slow to anger and abounding in mercy, and one who relents concerning threatened judgment. **4:3** So now, LORD, kill me instead, because I would rather die than live!" **4:4** The LORD said, "Are you really so very angry?"

4:5 Jonah left the city and sat down east of it. He made a shelter for himself there and sat down under it in the shade to see what would happen to the city. **4:6** The LORD God appointed a little plant and caused it to grow up over Jonah to be a shade over his head to rescue him from his misery. Now Jonah was very delighted about the little plant.

4:7 So God sent a worm at dawn the next day, and it attacked the little plant so that it dried up. **4:8** When the sun began to shine, God sent a hot east wind. So the sun beat down on Jonah's head, and he grew faint. So he despaired of life, and said, "I would rather die than live!" **4:9** God said to Jonah, "Are you really so very angry about the little plant?" And he said, "I am as angry as I could possibly be!" **4:10** The LORD said, "You were upset about this little plant, something for which you have not worked nor did you do anything to make it grow. It grew up overnight and died the next day. **4:11** Should I not be even more concerned about Nineveh, this enormous city? There are more than one hundred twenty thousand people in it who do not know right from wrong, as well as many animals!"

2. What stood out to you in your reading?

_____

_____

_____

3. What does the text reveal about God's character?

_____

_____

_____

4. What does the text reveal about humanity?

_____

_____

_____

TUESDAY: TRUE OR TRUTH?

1. Reread Jonah 1. As you read, bear in mind that Samaria, where Jonah lived, has a higher elevation than Joppa, where Jonah caught the boat. Going down to Joppa, down into the ship, down in the

hold—all this going down gives us something like stage direction to show us the depth of Jonah's spiritual rebellion.

1:1 The LORD said to Jonah son of Amittai, **1:2** "Go immediately to Nineveh, that large capital city, and announce judgment against its people because their wickedness has come to my attention." **1:3** Instead, Jonah immediately headed off to Tarshish to escape from the commission of the LORD. He traveled to Joppa and found a merchant ship heading to Tarshish. So he paid the fare and went aboard it to go with them to Tarshish far away from the LORD. **1:4** But the LORD hurled a powerful wind on the sea. Such a violent tempest arose on the sea that the ship threatened to break up! **1:5** The sailors were so afraid that each cried out to his own god and they flung the ship's cargo overboard to make the ship lighter. Jonah, meanwhile, had gone down into the hold below deck, had lain down, and was sound asleep. **1:6** The ship's captain approached him and said, "What are you doing asleep? Get up! Cry out to your god! Perhaps your god might take notice of us so that we might not die!" **1:7** The sailors said to one another, "Come on, let's cast lots to find out whose fault it is that this disaster has overtaken us. " So they cast lots, and Jonah was singled out. **1:8** They said to him, "Tell us, whose fault is it that this disaster has overtaken us? What's your occupation? Where do you come from? What's your country? And who are your people?" **1:9** He said to them, "I am a Hebrew! And I worship the LORD, the God of heaven, who made the sea and the dry land." **1:10** Hearing this, the men became even more afraid and said to him, "What have you done?" (The men said this because they knew that he was trying to escape from the LORD, because he had previously told them.) **1:11** Because the storm was growing worse and worse, they said to him, "What should we do to you to make the sea calm down for us?" **1:12** He said to them, "Pick me up and throw me into the sea to make the sea quiet down, because I know it's my fault you are in this severe storm." **1:13** Instead, they tried to row back to land, but they were not able to do so because the storm kept growing worse and worse. **1:14** So they cried out to the LORD, "Oh, please, LORD, don't let us die on account of this man! Don't hold us guilty of shedding innocent blood. After all, you, LORD, have done just as you pleased." **1:15** So they picked Jonah up and threw him into the sea, and the sea stopped raging. **1:16** The men feared the LORD greatly, and earnestly vowed to offer lavish sacrifices to the LORD.

1:17 The LORD sent a huge fish to swallow Jonah, and Jonah was in the stomach of the fish three days and three nights.

2. What was Jonah's father's name, according to Jonah 1:1?

3. What does the following passage from 2 Kings tell us about when and where Jonah lived and where he was from?

> **2 Kings 14:23** In the fifteenth year of the reign of Judah's King Amaziah, son of Joash, Jeroboam son of Joash became king over Israel. He reigned for forty-one years in Samaria. **14:24** He did evil in the sight of the Lord; he did not repudiate the sinful ways of Jeroboam son of Nebat who encouraged Israel to sin. **14:25** He restored the border of Israel from Lebo Hamath in the north to the sea of the Arabah in the south, in accordance with the word of the Lord God of Israel announced through his servant Jonah son of Amittai, the prophet from Gath Hepher. **14:26** The Lord saw Israel's intense suffering; everyone was weak and incapacitated and Israel had no deliverer. **14:27** The Lord had not decreed that he would blot out Israel's memory from under heaven, so he delivered them through Jeroboam son of Joash.

Jonah prophesied about the second King Jeroboam of Israel, who reigned from about 781–753 BC. The border he restored, described in 2 Kings 14:25, extended from modern north Syria to the Dead Sea. This means that the northern border of Israel expanded back to where it was under Solomon.

- *Gath Hepher.* The name of Jonah's hometown means literally "winepress of the pit." It's a small town on the boundary of Zebulun, about two miles from Nazareth.

4. So far we have the identity of Jonah's father, where Jonah lived, who reigned at the time, and where Jonah came from. In addition, Jesus made reference to Jonah. Read Matthew 12:38–42 and Luke 11:29–32.

Matthew 12:38–42 Then some of the experts in the law along with some Pharisees answered [Jesus], "Teacher, we want to see a sign from you." **12:39** But he answered them, "An evil and adulterous generation asks for a sign, but no sign will be given to it except the sign of the prophet Jonah. **12:40** For just as Jonah was in the belly of the huge fish for three days and three nights, so the Son of Man will be in the heart of the earth for three days and three nights. **12:41** The people of Nineveh will stand up at the judgment with this generation and condemn it, because they repented when Jonah preached to them—and now, something greater than Jonah is here! **12:42** The queen of the South will rise up at the judgment with this generation and condemn it, because she came from the ends of the earth to hear the wisdom of Solomon—and now, something greater than Solomon is here!"

Luke 11:29–32 As the crowds were increasing, Jesus began to say, "This generation is a wicked generation; it looks for a sign, but no sign will be given to it except the sign of Jonah. **11:30** For just as Jonah became a sign to the people of Nineveh, so the Son of Man will be a sign to this generation. **11:31** The queen of the South will rise up at the judgment with the people of this generation and condemn them, because she came from the ends of the earth to hear the wisdom of Solomon—and now, something greater than Solomon is here! **11:32** The people of Nineveh will stand up at the judgment with this generation and condemn it, because they repented when Jonah preached to them—and now, something greater than Jonah is here!

At a women's retreat at a ranch near Estes Park, Colorado, a woman told me, "I'm unsure about the Bible because six men decided what had to go and what stayed. It raises a lot of questions." Never mind that what she said was untrue. In recent years, books, movies, and news reports have popularized such misconceptions. Rather than wave them off as silly liberal subjects, we need to explore them. Perhaps no book of the Bible receives more criticism in terms of its authenticity than the Book of Jonah. For a clear, credible exploration about Bible manuscripts, check out Reinventing Jesus *by J. Ed Komoszewski, M. James Sawyer, and Daniel B. Wallace.*

5. What parallel did Jesus make between himself and Jonah?

_____

_____

_____

6. What contrast did Jesus make between the Pharisees (Matt. 12:38) and the Ninevites (v. 41), and what did the queen of Sheba (v. 42) have in common with the Ninevites?

_____

_____

_____

7. Go back through the Book of Jonah and identify all the miracles you find in it. List them here:

_____

_____

_____

_____

8. Why do you think many people deny the miracles in the Bible?

_____

_____

_____

_____

In the end, it's not about the cold-water vertebrate in this story, is it? Still, a lot of ink gets spilled on the subject of whether a human can survive in the stomach of a fish. In fact, studies in the Book of Jonah are often so focused on such details that the important stuff gets lost— that God has compassion for all people and that for the world to go on, his mercy must temper his justice.

Some, in a misguided effort to defend the faith, have cited relatively recent stories in which humans miraculously survived being eaten by fish and lived for several days. When such "fish stories" turn out to be exaggerated, however, they serve only to undermine the truth. Jesus refers to himself as "the truth" (John 14:6), and we must never lie or exaggerate in our attempts to glorify God. He has no need for us to stretch or fabricate stories to defend him and his Word!

Evangelical Old Testament scholar Dr. Robert Chisholm summarizes what's at stake here:

> Traditionally, the Book of Jonah has been understood as a historical account of an episode in the life of the prophet. Most modern scholars reject this notion and understand the book as legendary, allegorical, or parabolic. They argue that various elements in the book are too fantastic to be anything but fiction. For example, Jonah is preserved alive inside a large marine creature for three days and three nights and even prays (in beautiful Hebrew poetic verse) from the insides of the fish. When he preaches in Nineveh, which seems to be portrayed as much larger than it really was (see Jon. 3:3), the Ninevites repent en masse. Furthermore, secular history provides no evidence of such a spiritual revival among the Assyrians. . . . The debate over the book's historicity will undoubtedly continue, because for some it is a litmus test of orthodoxy that proves whether or not one is committed to historical Christianity. Surely such an attitude makes a philosophical 'mountain' out of a literary 'molehill.' Unlike the exodus and the resurrection of Jesus, the historicity of the Book of Jonah is not foundational to redemptive history and biblical faith."[3]

Consider also the words of Augustine: "What was prefigured by the prophet being swallowed by that monster and restored alive on the third day? Christ explained it when he said an evil and adulterous gen-

[3]Robert B. Chisholm, Jr., *Handbook on the Prophets* (Grand Rapids: Baker Academic, 2002), 407–408.

eration seeks a sign, and a sign shall not be given to it, but the sign of Jonah the prophet. For as Jonah was in the whale's belly three days and three nights, so shall the Son of man be in the heart of the earth three days and three nights."

We can learn something from both sides in this debate. First, we must cling to a high view of the Bible and the biblical perspective on miracles. Far more significant questions than whether Jonah's story is to be understood as nonfiction are these: Can God become a human? Can a man die and be raised three days later? In his book *Miracles*, C. S. Lewis wrote, "The Grand Miracle is about the story of the Incarnation—Jesus' life, death and resurrection. The whole of Christianity stems from this greatest miracle. The question is 'Am I to believe?' " Indeed, that is the question. If you don't believe in the miracle of the incarnation, it doesn't matter if you believe all the other miracles. So *could* the events in the Book of Jonah really happen? If God so desired—absolutely! Let there be no doubt about it.

Second, a word about inerrancy. To believe that every word of the Bible is true and inspired by God does not necessarily mean we must believe God intends for us to understand every word of it as nonfiction. Assuming otherwise is a mistake made by both believers and unbelievers. In fact, in an effort to undermine our faith, vocal unbelievers often read stories such as Jonah's and lay out their own requirements for what Christians *must* believe in order to be orthodox.

Jesus told parables. Some—believers and unbelievers—teach that his stories *had* to be nonfiction for Jesus to be an honest person. Otherwise, they say, he was lying. Such thinking makes a mockery of literary genres. Jesus' listeners, living in an oral culture, certainly understood storytelling. Perhaps a father really had a son who asked for his inheritance and then squandered it all (see Luke 15). But such a father didn't have to exist for Jesus to be honest or for characters to teach us that our heavenly Father is lavish in his love.

Some say that the speeches in the book of Job, all of which are written in excellent Hebrew poetry, had to have been literally spoken as written for the Bible to be accurate. That is, proponents of this idea think Job's friends had to talk in poetic speech for God's Word to be credible. Again, such an understanding misses the point of the Bible's fabulous literary qualities. God's Word is a fantastic compilation of nonfiction, history, narrative, poetry, apocalypse, parable, oracle, gospel—all of which creatively communicate God's trustworthy message. Name just about any genre, and the Bible has it.

One Bible teacher has written about the Book of Jonah, "The biblical account is a miraculous one. And we must remember to trust the Bible first and foremost, even if no other evidence supporting it exists." This writer is absolutely right. Yet a question the Book of Jonah raises is, What exactly is required in trusting the Bible in our approach to this book? Must we believe that God would never allow writers to recast stories in poetry or parable or novella? This is a completely different argument from that made by people who take a low view of Scripture and see all miracles as myths.

How we answer the novella-nonfiction question affects how we see this book. If Jonah's story is fiction on par with parables, a key focus of the story is the irony of Jonah's desire for God to judge everyone but himself. We read even the prayer in chapter 2 as ironic.

But if Jonah's story is nonfiction, Jonah himself is its most likely author. Tipping the scales toward this view is the fact that Jonah's father and hometown are mentioned and also that a real prophet named Jonah lived during this time. Assuming that Jonah wrote the book makes it both a narrative challenging readers to love their enemies and a wonderful redemption story. The prayer of praise in chapter 2 could be influenced by Jonah's change of heart and should be read as genuinely heartfelt—rather than ironic because of the events in chapter 4.

To keep the focus of this study on the author's main message—God's mercy and desire to relent in executing judgment—I've presented the issues raised by both sides of the novella-nonfiction question and will leave it for readers to decide. Know that people who hold to a high view of Scripture see it both ways.

9. Do you believe God is able to do miracles? Why or why not?

_____

_____

_____

10. What is your opinion about what you have just read?

_____

1. Reread Jonah 1:

> **1:1** The LORD said to Jonah son of Amittai, **1:2** "Go immediately to Nineveh, that large capital city, and announce judgment against its people because their wickedness has come to my attention." **1:3** Instead, Jonah immediately headed off to Tarshish to escape from the commission of the LORD. He traveled to Joppa and found a merchant ship heading to Tarshish. So he paid the fare and went aboard it to go with them to Tarshish far away from the LORD. **1:4** But the LORD hurled a powerful wind on the sea. Such a violent tempest arose on the sea that the ship threatened to break up! **1:5** The sailors were so afraid that each cried out to his own god and they flung the ship's cargo overboard to make the ship lighter. Jonah, meanwhile, had gone down into the hold below deck, had lain down, and was sound asleep. **1:6** The ship's captain approached him and said, "What are you doing asleep? Get up! Cry out to your god! Perhaps your god might take notice of us so that we might not die!" **1:7** The sailors said to one another, "Come on, let's cast lots to find out whose fault it is that this disaster has overtaken us." So they cast lots, and Jonah was singled out. **1:8** They said to him, "Tell us, whose fault is it that this disaster has overtaken us? What's your occupation? Where do you come from? What's your country? And who are your people?" **1:9** He said to them, "I am a Hebrew! And I worship the LORD, the God of heaven, who made the sea and the dry land." **1:10** Hearing this, the men became even more afraid and said to him, "What have you done?" (The men said this because they knew that he was trying to escape from the LORD, because he had previously told them.) **1:11** Because the storm was growing worse and worse, they said to him, "What should we do to you to make the sea calm down for us?" **1:12** He said to them, "Pick me up and throw me into the sea to make the sea quiet down, because I know it's my fault you are in this severe storm." **1:13** Instead, they tried to row back to land, but they were not able to do so because the storm kept growing worse and worse. **1:14** So they cried out to the LORD, "Oh, please, LORD, don't let us die on account of this man! Don't hold us guilty of shedding innocent blood. After all, you, LORD, have

done just as you pleased." **1:15** So they picked Jonah up and threw him into the sea, and the sea stopped raging. **1:16** The men feared the LORD greatly, and earnestly vowed to offer lavish sacrifices to the LORD.

1:17 The LORD sent a huge fish to swallow Jonah, and Jonah was in the stomach of the fish three days and three nights.

- *The LORD said* (1:1). When we see *LORD* in all capital letters in many English translations of the Bible such as this, the name for God in the underlying Hebrew text is YHWH, or *Yahweh*. *Lord* with lowercase letters generally means the name for God in the underlying text is Adonai. Whereas Adonai is the name for God as master, Yahweh refers to God as the self-existent one—"I am that I am" or "I will be that I will be." It's what God called Himself when Moses asked, "Whom shall I say has sent me?" Yahweh is the one who was, who is, and who is to come.

  We don't know how Jonah received his directions from the Lord. An angel could have appeared; a voice could have spoken from heaven; Jonah might have had a dream. Regardless of how God spoke, the important thing here is that Jonah *knew* what he was supposed to do.

- *Go immediately to Nineveh* (1:1). Jonah had commonsense reasons to resist going to Nineveh, the capital of the Neo-Assyrian Empire, Israel's archenemy. As mentioned, this empire threatened to destroy all that Jonah held dear. If the Ninevites repented in response to preaching, Jonah feared his actions could lead to the success of his enemies. Imagine you're a NATO soldier called to go help the Taliban, and you get a picture of Jonah's struggle.

  The city of Nineveh had a long and storied history. We find first mention of it in Genesis 10:11, where the text says Nimrod (a descendant of Ham from Noah) founded it. Our best guess is that Nineveh existed as early as 3000 BC. Scholars believe Nineveh got its name from Nina in South Babylonia on the Euphrates. From the *International Standard Bible Encyclopedia*, we learn that "the native name appears as Ninua or Nina (Ninaa), written with the character for 'water enclosure' with that for 'fish' inside, implying a connection between Nina and the Semitic nun, 'fish.' The Babylonian Nina was a place where fish were very abundant. . . . Fish are also plentiful in the Tigris at Mosul, the modern town on the other side of the river, and this may have influenced the choice of the site by the Babylonian settlers, and the foundation there of the great temple of Ishtar or Nina."[2] Remember this reference to the city being associated with fish; it will come up later.

* *That large capital* (1:2). The phrase could refer to Nineveh's largeness in size, greatness in renown, or relative number of citizens. At this time in history, Nineveh was the most powerful city in the ancient Near East. It lay more than five hundred miles from where Jonah lived—a long, long walk.

1. What are God's instructions to Jonah (1:2)?

_____

_____

_____

2. How does God describe Nineveh (1:2)?

_____

_____

_____

3. Read Nahum 3:1–19, which provides a description of Nineveh. Nahum the prophet spoke this prophecy against Nineveh about one hundred years after God commissioned Jonah.

Nahum 3:1 Woe to the city guilty of bloodshed!
She is full of lies;
she is filled with plunder;
she has hoarded her spoil!
3:2 The chariot drivers will crack their whips;
the chariot wheels will shake the ground;
the chariot horses will gallop;

[2]Ibid.

the war chariots will bolt forward!

3:3 The charioteers will charge ahead;
their swords will flash
and their spears will glimmer!
There will be many people slain;
there will be piles of the dead,
and countless casualties—
so many that people will stumble over the corpses.

3:4 "Because you have acted like a wanton prostitute—
a seductive mistress who practices sorcery,
who enslaves nations by her harlotry,
and entices peoples by her sorcery—

3:5 I am against you," declares the LORD who commands armies.
"I will strip off your clothes!
I will show your nakedness to the nations
and your shame to the kingdoms;

3:6 I will pelt you with filth;
I will treat you with contempt;
I will make you a public spectacle.

3:7 Everyone who sees you will turn away from you in disgust;
they will say, 'Nineveh has been devastated!
Who will lament for her?'
There will be no one to comfort you!"

3:8 You are no more secure than Thebes—
she was located on the banks of the Nile;
the waters surrounded her,
her rampart was the sea,
the water was her wall.

3:9 Cush and Egypt had limitless strength;
Put and the Libyans were among her allies.

3:10 Yet she went into captivity as an exile;
even her infants were smashed to pieces at the head of every
street.
They cast lots for her nobility;
all her dignitaries were bound with chains.

3:11 You too will act like drunkards;
you will go into hiding;
you too will seek refuge from the enemy.
3:12 All your fortifications will be like fig trees with first-ripe fruit:
If they are shaken, their figs will fall into the mouth of the eater!

....

3:19 Your destruction is like an incurable wound;
your demise is like a fatal injury!
All who hear what has happened to you will clap their hands for joy,
for no one ever escaped your endless cruelty!

1. How does Nahum's prophesy add to our understanding of what Nineveh must have been like?

_____

_____

_____

2. What reason does God give for his instructions to Jonah (Jon. 1:2)?

_____

_____

3. God says, "Their wickedness has come to my attention" (1:2). Do you think this means God was previously unaware of Nineveh's wickedness? Why or why not? What is God communicating about himself in this section?

_____

_____

_____

1. Pray for insight; then read Jonah 1:1–3:

> **Jonah 1:1** The LORD said to Jonah son of Amittai, **1:2** "Go immediately to Nineveh, that large capital city, and announce judgment against its people because their wickedness has come to my attention." **1:3** Instead, Jonah immediately headed off to Tarshish to escape from the commission of the LORD. He traveled to Joppa and found a merchant ship heading to Tarshish. So he paid the fare and went aboard it to go with them to Tarshish far away from the LORD.

1. List reasons you think Jonah had for resisting God's command.

_____

_____

_____

_____

2. What should Jonah have done? Why?

_____

_____

_____

3. In the Hebrew, God literally commands Jonah to "arise," and in verse 3 we read that Jonah did in fact "rise up." Yet where did he go and why?

_____

_____

_____

4. On the map below locate Jonah's hometown, where Jonah caught the boat, where Jonah was supposed to go, and where he headed.

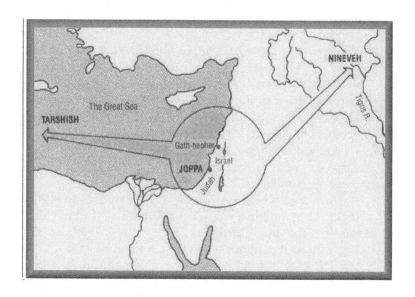

5. Has God ever directed you to do something you really did not want to do? If so, how did you respond?

_____

_____

_____

_____

6. The King James translation of Jonah 1:3 captures well the Hebrew author's use of *up* and *down*: "But Jonah rose up to flee unto Tarshish from the presence of the LORD, and went down to Joppa; and he found a ship going to Tarshish: so he paid the fare thereof, and went down into it, to go with them unto Tarshish from the presence of the LORD." What phrase is repeated twice in this verse?

- *He traveled to Joppa* (1:3). Joppa was a seaport in Jonah's day, just as it exists today as Jaffa, part of the municipality of Tel Aviv. For an Israelite in Jonah's day, Joppa represented the edge of the earth, so for Jonah to get on a ship is most remarkable. Hebrew people at this time shared the Canaanites' fear of the ocean; although they didn't consider the sea to be a god as the Canaanites did, they held a strongly negative view of it. For Jonah to hop on a boat and head out by way of the ominous ocean demonstrates his desperation to disobey.

  This becomes even more significant when we see Jonah lying sound asleep during a tempest that frightens even experienced sailors and is nearly strong enough to break the boat apart. Under normal circumstances, "the last thing he'd do is sleep," says Dr. Ronald B. Allen, professor of Old Testament at Dallas Theological Seminary. Taking into account that Jonah was probably afraid of the ocean, coupled with his spiritual turmoil, Allen believes Jonah was either drunk or drugged.

7. Read 1 Kings 10:21–22:

   1 Kings 10:21 All of King Solomon's cups were made of gold, and all the household items in the Palace of the Lebanon Forest were made of pure gold. There were no silver items, for silver was not considered very valuable in Solomon's time. **10:22** Along with Hiram's fleet, the king had a fleet of large merchant ships* 35 that sailed the sea. Once every three years the fleet came into port with cargoes of gold, silver, ivory, apes, and peacocks.

   Now go back to Monday's section where you find the entire Book of Jonah and circle the number of times *Tarshish* appears.

8. *Tarshish* is a Sanscrit or Aryan word meaning "the sea coast." Some think the Tarshish in the book of Jonah is a location on the Indian coast. Others think Tarshish is another name for Carthage. A more

---

* The Hebrew here says "a fleet of Tarshish [ships]."

probable option, however, is that it's a Phoenician port in Spain with abundant gold and silver mines. The phrase "ships of Tarshish" may also have been an expression used to describe ships intended and outfitted for a long voyage, similar to how we might say, "This afternoon I went to outer Siberia." After reading the description of Tarshish, what do you think might have made it attractive to Jonah?

_____

_____

_____

9. What attractions, exotic or otherwise, pull *you* down and away from what you know God wants you to do?

_____

_____

_____

10. Spend some time praying that God will enable you to trust his heart and resist the attractions that pull you in the wrong direction.

FRIDAY: STORMY WEATHER

1. Pray for the Holy Spirit to grant you insight; then read Jonah 1:4–7.

Jonah 1:4 But the LORD hurled a powerful wind on the sea. Such a violent tempest arose on the sea that the ship threatened to break up! **1:5** The sailors were so afraid that each cried out to his own god and they flung the ship's cargo overboard to make the ship lighter. Jonah, meanwhile, had gone down into the hold below deck, had lain down, and was sound asleep. **1:6** The ship's captain approached him and said, "What are you doing asleep? Get up! Cry out to your god! Perhaps your god might take notice of us so that we might not die!" **1:7** The sailors said to one another, "Come on, let's cast lots to find out whose fault it is that this disaster has overtaken us." So they cast lots, and Jonah was singled out.

2. Describe the source and strength of the wind (1:4). What does this indicate about the scope and strength of God's power?

_____

_____

_____

- *Such a violent tempest arose on the sea that the ship threatened to break up!* (1:4). The Hebrew text here literally says, "The ship thought [it] would be broken"; the writer portrays the ship as if it has human qualities. The Book of Jonah is full of such poetic elements. Here the literary elements serve to doubly emphasize the absolute strength of the storm.

2. What did the sailors do in response to the storm's violence (1:5)? How does this compare with Jonah's reaction?

_____

_____

_____

3. What's ironic about this contrast?

_____

_____

_____

4. Use your imagination to picture the scene—the taste of salt water, the violence of being jarred and tossed, the terror of drowning, the rain pelting your face, the sound of the wind. Describe your impressions.

_____

_____

_____

_____

_____

_____

> Phoenicians controlled shipping in the Mediterranean during the Israelite monarchy, so the sailors in this story were likely Phoenician. Their major cities were Tyre and Sidon. If so, they probably lived on the northern coast of modern-day Lebanon.

5. Consider that Jonah slept because he was, at the heart of it, failing to trust God. Yet when Jesus slept in a boat during a storm, his rest indicated his trust in God (Matt. 8:23–27). What can we observe from these two examples?

_____

_____

_____

6. What does the shipmaster say to Jonah (1:6)?

_____

_____

_____

_____

7. Only four verses earlier we read what God said. A literal Hebrew rendering is, "Get up! Go to Nineveh . . . . and *cry out*" (v. 2, italics added). When you compare what God said with the shipmaster's words, what is sadly ironic?

_____

_____

_____

8. The sailors rightly assumed that such a storm—the likes of which even they had never seen—was the result of someone angering his god. They cast lots to determine the offending party, and the results correctly pointed to Jonah (1:7). Unlike other forms of divination, casting lots was not prohibited in Israel. In the book of 1 Samuel, we find a story in which God refrains from answering a request by Saul, so the king casts lots to discover who sinned (14:41–42). In the Book of Esther, God supervised the casting of lots to set a date for the destruction of the Jews. (The word *purim*, after which Esther's feast is named, means "lots.") And the eleven disciples cast lots to determine Judas's successor. We don't know exactly what people used for lots. Whether they used a black bean, drew straws, rolled dice, or used some other method, however, the point is clear: God worked through an apparently random event to communicate something. What does the result of the sailors' casting lots tell you about God?

_____

_____

_____

- *This disaster has overtaken us* (1:7). The Hebrew word *ra'ah*, translated here as "disaster," is the same word rendered as "wickedness" five verses earlier:

  1:1 The LORD said to Jonah son of Amittai, **1:2** "Go immediately to Nineveh, that large capital city, and announce judgment against its people because their **wickedness** has come to my attention." (emphasis added)

  ....

  1:7 The sailors said to one another, "Come on, let's cast lots to find out whose fault it is that this **disaster** has overtaken us." So they cast lots, and Jonah was singled out. (emphasis added)

In its first usage the word means evil in its moral sense, and in the second instance it means the consequences of evil. We use the English word *evil* similarly to express such a double meaning: "Stop doing evil, or a great evil will happen to you." Note again the irony here—the one whom God sent to announce doom to those deserving it ends up dooming those who don't.

9. What evidences of God's sovereignty do you see in this story so far?

_____

_____

_____

10. The lost sailors prayed while the prophet Jonah slept. Do you ever act less righteously than unbelievers around you? Do you ever hear people claim to walk in the faith whose actions are more sinful than those who don't claim faith? List examples (no names, please).

_____

_____

_____

11. Write out a prayer asking for help to glorify God in how you live and to follow the Lord's commands no matter what the cost.

_____

_____

_____

Saturday: Translation Sensation

Jeff Wofford, one of my writing students, described himself as "absolutely giddy" upon completing his first-ever Hebrew translation on the beginning of Jonah. The reason, he said, was that such translating added color to his understanding. He loved finding out that the word we render "to sleep deeply" (1:5) can simply mean "to snore." He also noted:

> I began to see connections I hadn't noticed before. Jonah is an underachiever. Both God and the ship captain have to tell

him to "get up!" People keep throwing things: God throws a wind on the sea, prompting the sailors to throw their stuff overboard. Later, they'll cast lots, and then of course they'll chuck Jonah. The star of the show is kind of a lovable nut. What is more comical—and yet disturbingly believable—than a prophet who thinks he can escape from God? What kind of weird mix of faith and rebellion would enable someone to sleep through the perfect storm?

Yet Jeff's more profound observations come not from the text's little details, interesting as they are; they came from what he discovered after putting them all together: "Jonah is more than a slapstick crank, and much more than a children's book character. The tension that drives him is one that drives me. On the one hand, he wants to serve people and bring them closer to God. On the other hand, he thinks God is too good for those people—and by implication, so is he. It's easy to hold contempt for those you're sent to serve."

The prophet Jonah has some clear issues with bigotry, nationalism, rebellion, and gracelessness. We see some of these same issues in the book of Esther with Haman, who hates Mordecai because he's Jewish. And we see Paul addressing the divisions caused by such thinking in the first-century church: he tells of how in Christ we are not to allow labels like Greek, Jew, circumcised, barbarian, Scythian, slave, or free to divide us (see Col. 3:11).

While it's true that Israel was chosen by God then and Christians are chosen by God now, we should not understand *chosen* as a synonym for *favorite*. The point of our "chosen-ness" is as a means to an end—so we can shine as light for those to whom God wants to demonstrate love. With our exalted state comes a call to share it with all who will respond.

And that is precisely what hacked Jonah off. He wanted to hoard God's favor for himself. He resented God's compassion toward the enemy. Jonah saw the evil in the Assyrians' actions, yet he failed to see hatred's subtler form lurking in his own heart.

Such evil has nothing to do with education. We have seen it from remote warring Amazonian tribes to highly cultured Germans designing extermination camps. It's present in every culture, in every community, in every human heart.

We are all both the objects and subjects of violations when it comes to human dignity. At the height of the 2008 presidential campaign *New York Times* columnist Nicholas Kristof observed, "At a New York or Los Angeles cocktail party, few would dare make a pejorative comment about Barack Obama's race or Hillary Clinton's sex. Yet it would be easy to get away with deriding Mike Huckabee's religious faith. Liberals believe deeply in tolerance and over the last century have led the battles against prejudices of all kinds, but we have a blind spot about Christian evangelicals."

True enough.

Yet he doesn't let Christ-followers off the hook either: "Moralizing blowhards showed more compassion for embryonic stem cells than for the poor or the sick."

Sadly, he was right. That's *not* to say we should hold a low view of humans in their one-cell state. But sanctity of life extends from embryo and unborn baby to active euthanasia, nuclear bombs, murder in Sudan, eugenics, unlimited in vitro fertilization, the disposability of girls in China, and Indian widows expected to kill themselves when their husbands die—to name a few. Human dignity, grounded in God's creation of humanity, has ramifications beyond the unborn. It extends to sex trafficking, torture, hydration for people in vegetative states, slavery, POW standards, immigration policy, homelessness, poverty, and hunger.

We like our own causes best; we like our own country best; we like our denomination best; we like our own families best; we prefer the schools we attended, the neighborhoods where we grew up, our own political party or cause, our gender—even our brand of peanut butter. And somewhere along the way we cross the line from preference to prejudice. We pray for our loved ones but rarely, if ever, our enemies. Mention atheists, humanists, materialists, homosexuals, and radical feminists in most churches today, and you can believe the response you'll evoke will sound nothing like, "Let's pray right now for God to pour out his love."

Genesis tells us that humans are fellow creations of one maker, and that means we must view and treat each other as such. The qualities of God that so angered Jonah are the very qualities we most need: grace, compassion, patience, mercy, abundant love, and truth. And not just for those we love—but for those we hate. For those who have wronged us. For those who want us dead. The only possible way we can demonstrate such remarkable goodness is through the power of the Holy Spirit.

On our own, we are all Jonahs at heart.

Our only hope is to be cast overboard and stranded on Omnipotence.

Pray: *Heavenly Father, thank you for your grace! You poured out your favor on me, even when I was still your enemy lost in sin. Help me to show that same grace to those who don't yet know you. Help me to love my enemies, to act graciously with those who want to destroy all I hold dear, to pray for those who persecute me. Thank you that you are sovereign over everything and that you can use anything, anytime, from ocean waves to dice. Grant me an obedient heart to follow you fully and to trust you completely. Please make me like you—gracious, compassionate, slow to anger, abounding in mercy. In the name of your Son, who brought reconciliation, amen.*

Memorize: "You are gracious and compassionate, slow to anger and abounding in mercy, and one who relents concerning threatened judgment" (Jon. 4:2).

Week 2 of 4

Praying from the Gut: Jonah 1:8–2:10

Scripture: I called out to the LORD from my distress, and he answered me; from the belly of Sheol I cried out for help, and you heard my prayer (Jon. 2:2).

When I was in the beautiful Hashemite Kingdom of Jordan in 2008, I stood in an amphitheater with excellent acoustics. My kind Muslim guide directed me to the best spot for amplification and told me to say or sing something. Do you know what came to mind? A song with lyrics right out of 1 Thessalonians that I learned three decades earlier. Music has a way of staying in memory, doesn't it, more than words alone?

So I shot up a prayer for courage and boldly recited the lyrics, which include, "If we believe that Jesus died and rose again, even so those also who sleep in Jesus will God bring with him." There I was, referring to the key facts of the gospel in a place where it's illegal to proselytize. Yet the officials, standing openmouthed, allowed it

31

because I was "giving a recitation" rather than delivering a message. I never could have done that if I'd tried to formulate my own words on the spot!

What have you memorized? Perhaps you know more than you think. See if you can complete any or all of these phrases from the book of Psalms:

1) The LORD is my shepherd, I . . .
2) My God, my God, why . . .
3) What is man that you are mindful of him or . . .
4) Not to us, O Lord, but to your name . . .
5) I lift up my eyes to the hills. From where does my . . .

If you answered: 1) shall not want; 2) have you forsaken me?; 3) the son of man that you visit him?; 4) give glory; and 5) help come from?—or similar phrasing, depending on your translation—you had it right.

These lines come from some of the best-known psalms. And up until about the last one hundred years, many—if not most—Christ-followers could have completed hundreds of such phrases, because believers often turned to the psalms for their morning and evening meditations. Today, however, if we even spend time regularly in the Word, most of us use a variety of devotional books. The demand for such works rises and falls, but in general a huge market exists for them. So we've moved away from the psalms in our daily reading. (Fortunately, at the same time, we sing many psalms as praise songs.)

When Jonah found himself in the belly of the fish, he prayed. And when we take a close look at his prayer, we find he was fluent in "Psalmese," as he composed his words from a variety of works from the Bible's book of Psalms. Compiled several hundred years before his birth, Psalms would have been Jonah's prayer book, and at a time when Jonah had no written scroll handy, he recalled what he already knew.

We also see recitations from the psalms on the lips of Mary and Jesus. And while many Christians consider prewritten prayers to be empty rituals (there *is* a danger in saying prayers only by rote), we don't have to go to such extremes. Consider these words from a friend:

> I've had some difficulty with prayer. Thus, I've been rec-
> ognizing how Christians in past times have used the psalms as
> their prayers, and I've been encouraged to spend some time

reading Psalms. (I'd always been taught, growing up, that a prayer wasn't sincere unless it was my own spontaneous, original words, and I have very few of those!) Tonight I ran across one that really expressed what I wanted to say to God. It's in Psalm 25, particularly these verses:

To you, O LORD , I lift up my soul (v. 1).

Show me your ways, O LORD, teach me your paths (v. 4).

Guide me in your truth and teach me; for you are God my savior, and my hope is in you all day long (v. 5).

The troubles of my heart have multiplied; free me from my anguish (v. 17).

Look upon my affliction and distress and take away all my sins (v. 18).

I guess the "spiritual" thing to say is that I had a "confident peace" with the prayer as I tried to express it to God. But I'll just say that I felt good about it, something that doesn't often happen when I pray.

This same woman went on to say that she found the following written-out prayer, and it meant a lot to her:

Dear Lord, how the love of my friends towards me rejoices my heart. Who can describe the feeling of the heart that comes from knowing people's love? It is indescribable. To be aware that there are people who love me, even as the miserable sinner that I am, fills me with hope. And the source of the hope is the knowledge that my friends' love for me is a pale shadow of God's love for me. Thus when God takes me to heaven, the present joy I have in friendship will be multiplied a thousand-fold.— John Sergieff, *Book of Prayers*

> You can find two psalms in a piece of classical music, Handel's Messiah: Psalm 2—"Why Do the Nations Rage?" and Psalm 24—"Lift Up Your Head, O Ye Gates." If you're completing this study as part of a group, tell each other your favorite psalm tunes. What do you recommend?

Jonah's prayer offered from the belly of the fish is both structured and spontaneous. The words come preformed from existing psalms, but Jonah chose his stanzas from a smattering of sources, all of which formed a whole to meet the need of the moment. In short,

Jonah voiced a spontaneous prayer using preformed wording that fit the situation.

Why not give it a try yourself? As part of studying Jonah, try learning some psalms. But do it the easy way—learn some psalms set to music.

What's in your cassette, CD, or MP3 player? Why not download or purchase some music based on the psalms so you can commit to memory a variety of expressions that cover the range of human emotions? When Jesus hung on the cross, he recited a line from a psalm of David—"My God, my God, why have you forsaken me?" (Ps. 22:1, NIV). In echoing such psalms, we find timeless words with which to approach the timeless, ever-present Lord who welcomes the sound of his needy child's voice.

MONDAY: JONAH OUTED

1. Pray for insight; then read the following from the Book of Jonah:

> **Jonah 1:8** [The sailors] said to him, "Tell us, whose fault is it that this disaster has overtaken us? What's your occupation? Where do you come from? What's your country? And who are your people?" **1:9** He said to them, "I am a Hebrew! And I worship the LORD, the God of heaven, who made the sea and the dry land." **1:10** Hearing this, the men became even more afraid and said to him, "What have you done?" (The men said this because they knew that he was trying to escape from the LORD, because he had previously told them.)

2. What do the sailors ask Jonah (1:8)?

_____

_____

3. Based on information given in your earlier reading, answer the sailors' questions:

What was Jonah's occupation?

_____

What was Jonah's home town?

_____

What were Jonah's country and heritage?

_____

- *I worship the* LORD, *the God of heaven, who made the sea and the dry land* (1:9). The word translated "worship" here is actually the word *fear*. Jonah claims to "fear" the Lord, yet his actions demonstrate anything but. Ironically, we will later see the sailors fear the Lord greatly (v. 16), and instead of rebellion, their fear leads to actions—vows and sacrifices to the true God. Jonah should fear God—the God of the sea!—to the point that he obeys. He should fear the storm to the point that he wakes up and at least helps the sailors chuck cargo overboard. While many theologians downplay the concept of the fear of God to keep from terrorizing people, the reality is that a holy reverence that makes us quake is not necessarily a bad thing. As my pastor likes to remind us, "Jesus is not your homeboy."

  When my daughter was three or four years old, she would run off the end of the diving board into the pool. We had to remain vigilant when she went swimming because she would run headlong into danger, lacking the healthy fear many children have of water. We sometimes wished she were a more fearful child!

  Each of us should fear that which is truly dangerous. But Jonah demonstrates a callousness in both the physical and spiritual realms about things that should make him tremble.

4. How do the sailors respond to Jonah's answers (1:10–11)?

_____

_____

_____

_____

5. What does Jonah advise the sailors to do (1:12)?

_____

_____

_____

6. Based on his knowledge of God's desire, what should Jonah have advised (see Jon. 1:1)?

_____

_____

Jonah would rather drown than give the citizens of Nineveh an opportunity to fear God! Notice that Jonah does not pray or repent here. And remember this death wish—Jonah will have another one before his story is over.

7. What does Jonah say about his God (1:9–10)?

_____

_____

_____

8. Contrast the sailors' fear of Yahweh with Jonah's. What's incongruent here?

_____

_____

_____

9. Make a list of some of the many places where God is. (Use separate sheet of paper if necessary.) If you're an artsy type, make a collage of

photos or magazine pictures that remind you of the myriad places where God can be found.

---

10. In the decades that followed the life of Christ, the apostle Paul entered Athens. When he looked around, he saw altars *everywhere*. Athena, Zeus, Artemis, emperors—all over. He even spotted one altar dedicated to an unknown God. Rather than rail on Athens's citizens for their polytheism, he observed something about God—something similar to what we see in Jonah's failed attempt to run away from him. Ask the Spirit for insight; then read the account:

> **Acts 17:16** While Paul was waiting for them in Athens, his spirit was greatly upset because he saw the city was full of idols. **17:17** So he was addressing the Jews and the God-fearing Gentiles in the synagogue, and in the marketplace every day those who happened to be there. **17:18** Also some of the Epicurean and Stoic philosophers were conversing with him, and some were asking, "What does this foolish babbler want to say?" Others said, "He seems to be a proclaimer of foreign gods." (They said this because he was proclaiming the good news about Jesus and the resurrection.) **17:19** So they took Paul and brought him to the Areopagus, saying, "May we know what this new teaching is that you are proclaiming? **17:20** For you are bringing some surprising things to our ears, so we want to know what they mean." **17:21** (All the Athenians and the foreigners who lived there used to spend their time in nothing else than telling or listening to something new.)
>
> **17:22** So Paul stood before the Areopagus and said, "Men of Athens, I see that you are very religious in all respects. **17:23** For as I went around and observed closely your objects of worship, I even found an altar with this inscription: 'To an unknown god.' Therefore what you worship without knowing it, this I proclaim to you. **17:24** The God who made the world and everything in it, who is Lord of heaven and earth, does not live in temples made by human hands, **17:25** nor is he served by human hands, as if he needed anything, because he himself gives life and breath and everything to everyone. **17:26** From one man he made every nation of the human race

to inhabit the entire earth, determining their set times and the fixed limits of the places where they would live, **17:27** so that they would search for God and perhaps grope around for him and find him, though he is not far from each one of us. **17:28** For in him we live and move about and exist, as even some of your own poets have said, 'For we too are his offspring.' **17:29** So since we are God's offspring, we should not think the deity is like gold or silver or stone, an image made by human skill and imagination. **17:30** Therefore, although God has overlooked such times of ignorance, he now commands all people everywhere to repent, **17:31** because he has set a day on which he is going to judge the world in righteousness, by a man whom he designated, having provided proof to everyone by raising him from the dead."

What common elements about God's presence do we find in both Jonah's story and in Paul's message?

_____

_____

11. Why do you think the sailors in Jonah's story considered it risky to attempt an escape from the one who made the heaven, dry land, and sea?

_____

_____

_____

_____

12. Consider your own life. If you truly believed God is everywhere and sees all, how might it change you?

_____

_____

_____

13. Pray for the Lord to show you the incongruities between what you believe and the way you're living. Ask him to empower you to change.

_____

_____

_____

TUESDAY: JONAH OUSTED

1. Pray for insight; then read the following passage:

> **Jonah 1:10–16** Hearing this, the men became even more afraid and said to him, "What have you done?" (The men said this because they knew that he was trying to escape from the LORD, because he had previously told them.) **1:11** Because the storm was growing worse and worse, they said to him, "What should we do to you to make the sea calm down for us?" **1:12** He said to them, "Pick me up and throw me into the sea to make the sea quiet down, because I know it's my fault you are in this severe storm." **1:13** Instead, they tried to row back to land, but they were not able to do so because the storm kept growing worse and worse. **1:14** So they cried out to the LORD, "Oh, please, LORD, don't let us die on account of this man! Don't hold us guilty of shedding innocent blood. After all, you, LORD, have done just as you pleased." **1:15** So they picked Jonah up and threw him into the sea, and the sea stopped raging. **1:16** The men feared the LORD greatly, and earnestly vowed to offer lavish sacrifices to the LORD.

2. List the things that evoked fear in its various forms (whether stated or implied) in the sailors in this passage.

_____

_____

_____

_____

3. How did the sailors respond (vv. 13–15) to Jonah's suggestion to "throw me into the sea"? Do you see anything to admire in their choices?

_____

_____

_____

4. Jonah placed at risk the lives of the sailors, yet they desired to show him mercy. Compare and contrast these sailors' desire to save Jonah— one man—with his lack of desire to take God's message to Nineveh— a city of more than ten thousand people. What's wrong with this picture?

_____

_____

_____

5. The sailors exclaimed in horror, "Why have you done this?" List all the people affected by Jonah's bad choices.

_____

_____

_____

6. Have you ever been affected by someone's disobedience? If so, share the circumstances. (No names, please.)

_____

_____

_____

7. Use your sanctified imagination: How would it feel to be Jonah, knowing his disobedience has led to others' trauma and his own destruction? How would it feel to be a sailor having to cast someone into the sea to save your own life? What would it be like to watch the water instantly become calm after doing so? Jot down your thoughts.

_____

_____

_____

8. What evidences of true faith do you see in the sailors as they react to the storm ending (1:16)?

_____

_____

_____

9. What name for deity did the sailors use when they prayed, offered sacrifices, and made vows (especially v. 16)? (Describing someone as having a "fear of the Lord" is an Old Testament way of saying someone believes in the true God. We see several such examples of Gentiles coming to faith throughout the Old Testament.)

_____

_____

10. What does the description of these sailors suggest about how God used even Jonah's disobedience as an opportunity to show his mercy to outsiders?

_____

_____

_____

11. What does it tell you about God that he used Jonah's disobedience to demonstrate his power to these sailors?

_____

_____

_____

12. Interact with this statement: God can't use you if you're failing to live an obedient life. True or false? Explain your answer.

_____

_____

_____

WEDNESDAY: HARD TO SWALLOW

1. Pray for insight. Then read this portion of Jonah's story:

> **Jonah 1:11** Because the storm was growing worse and worse, they said to [Jonah], "What should we do to you to make the sea calm down for us?" **1:12** He said to them, "Pick me up and throw me into the sea to make the sea quiet down, because I know it's my fault you are in this severe storm." **1:13** Instead, they tried to row back to land, but they were not able to do so because the storm kept growing worse and worse. **1:14** So they cried out to the LORD, "Oh, please, LORD, don't let us die on account of this man! Don't hold us guilty of shedding innocent blood. After all, you, LORD, have done just as you pleased." **1:15** So they picked Jonah up and threw him into the sea, and the sea stopped raging. **1:16** The men feared the LORD greatly, and earnestly vowed to offer lavish sacrifices to the LORD. **1:17** The LORD sent a huge fish to swallow Jonah, and Jonah was in the stomach of the fish three days and three nights.

2. Envision yourself as one of the sailors and tell a friend about the trip, the storm, the Hebrew Jonah, and your new worship experience. Write this in a brief paragraph.

_____

_____

_____

_____

_____

3. A lot of this story hinges on one small verse—Jonah 1:17. What did the sailors think would happen when they threw Jonah overboard? Contrast this with what actually happened.

_____

_____

_____

4. To get the most out of Bible study, we need to keep in mind the audience that originally received the message. Imagine you're in the audience hearing this story for the first time. How might you respond to the reversal of events?

_____

_____

_____

5. What does it tell you about God that he sent a fish to swallow Jonah, saving his life? Why do you think he did it?

_____

_____

_____

6. Imagine sailors tossing you overboard into a raging sea. What would you expect to happen next? Picture a giant fish (we're not told it's a whale) eating you. How would that feel? What do you think it would be like to feel the temperature, inhale the smells, burn in the digestive juices, press against the bones, slosh against the other stomach contents? Do you imagine it's tight in there? Jot your ideas here.

_____

_____

_____

7. What might you say to God (if anything!) if this happened to you and you had three days to think about it? Would you be relieved? Still terrified? What do you think went through Jonah's mind?

_____

_____

- *In the stomach of the fish three days and three nights* (1:17). The time given here could indicate how far from dry land the ship had traveled from the departure point and thus the time it took the fish to return to Joppa. Another option is that people living in the ancient Near East in Jonah's day viewed a trip to the underworld as a three-day journey, so this could be a literary way of expressing a parallel motif for the trip back. A third option, which could be combined with the first, is that the fish traveled to the point on the coast closest to Nineveh to facilitate Jonah's journey there (see map from week 1).

8. Have you ever tried to run from God and been stopped? Or have you ever known someone else who did? What happened?

_____

_____

_____

In his brilliant work on the Book of Jonah, *Under the Unpredictable Plant: An Exploration of Vocational Holiness*, Eugene Peterson writes, "That Jonah prayed is not remarkable; we commonly pray when we are in desperate circumstances. But there is something very remarkable about the way Jonah prayed. He prayed a 'set' prayer. Jonah's prayer is not spontaneously original self-expression. It is totally derivative. Jonah had been to school to learn to pray, and he prayed as he had been taught. His school was the Psalms."[4]

1. Ask the Holy Spirit to grant you insight into the text; then read Jonah 1:17–2:10:

1:17 The LORD sent a huge fish to swallow Jonah, and Jonah was in the stomach of the fish three days and three nights.

2:1 Jonah prayed to the LORD his God from the stomach of the fish

2:2 and said, "I called out to the LORD from my distress,

and he answered me;

from the belly of Sheol I cried out for help,

and you heard my prayer.

2:3 You threw me into the deep waters,

into the middle of the sea;

the ocean current engulfed me;

all the mighty waves you sent swept over me.

2:4 I thought I had been banished from your sight,

that I would never again see your holy temple!

2:5 Water engulfed me up to my neck;

the deep ocean surrounded me;

seaweed was wrapped around my head.

2:6 I went down to the very bottoms of the mountains;

the gates of the netherworld barred me in forever;

but you brought me up from the Pit, O LORD, my God.

---

[4]Eugene Peterson, *Under the Unpredictable Plant: An Exploration of Vocational Holiness* (Grand Rapids: Eerdmans, 1992), 100.

2:7 When my life was ebbing away, I called out to the LORD, and my prayer came to your holy temple.

2:8 Those who worship worthless idols forfeit the mercy that could be theirs.

2:9 But as for me, I promise to offer a sacrifice to you with a public declaration of praise;

I will surely do what I have promised.

Salvation belongs to the LORD!"

2:10 Then the LORD commanded the fish and it disgorged Jonah on dry land.

Some favorite books containing prayers:
The Book of Psalms
The Book of Common Prayer
Valley of Vision: A Collection of Puritan Prayers and Devotions, *edited by Arthur G. Bennett*

2. Compare Jonah 2:2 with the psalms below. What similarities do you see?

Jonah **2:2** "I called out to the LORD from my distress, and he answered me; from the belly of Sheol, I cried out for help, and you heard my prayer.

Psalm **18:6** In my distress I called to the LORD; I cried out to my God. From his heavenly temple he heard my voice; he listened to my cry for help.

Psalm **120:1** In my distress I cried out to the LORD and he answered me.

Psalm **86:13** For you will extend your great loyal love to me, and will deliver my life from the depths of Sheol.

_____

_____

_____

3. Compare Jonah 2:3 with the psalms below. What similarities do you see?

Jonah **2:3** You threw me into the deep waters, into the middle of the sea; the ocean current engulfed me; all the mighty waves you sent swept over me.

Psalm 69:1, 2 Deliver me, O God, for the water has reached my neck. I sink into the deep mire where there is no solid ground; I am in deep water, and the current overpowers me.

Psalm 69:14 Rescue me from the mud! Don't let me sink! Deliver me from those who hate me, from the deep water!

Psalm 88:6 You place me in the lowest regions of the pit, in the dark places, in the watery depths.

Psalm 42:7 One deep stream calls out to another at the sound of your waterfalls; all your billows and waves overwhelm me.

---

4. Compare Jonah 2:4 with the verse from Psalms below. What similarities do you see?

Jonah 2:4 I thought I had been banished from your sight, that I would never again see your holy temple!

Psalm 31:22 I jumped to conclusions and said, "I am cut off from your presence!" But you heard my plea for mercy when I cried out to you for help.

---

5. Compare Jonah 2:5 with the verse from Psalms below. What similarities do you see?

Jonah 2:5 Water engulfed me up to my neck; the deep ocean surrounded me; seaweed was wrapped around my head.

Psalm 69:1, 2 Deliver me, O God, for the water has reached my neck. I sink into the deep mire where there is no solid ground; I am in deep water, and the current overpowers me.

6. Compare Jonah 2:6 with the verses from Psalms below. What similarities do you see?

Jonah 2:6 I went down to the very bottoms of the mountains; the gates of the netherworld barred me in forever; but you brought me up from the Pit, O Lord, my God.

Psalm 30:3 O LORD, you pulled me up from Sheol; you rescued me from among those descending into the grave.

Psalm 16:10 You will not abandon me to Sheol; you will not allow your faithful follower to see the Pit.

Psalm 18:5 The ropes of Sheol tightened around me, the snares of death trapped me.

> *Herbert Butterfield, the Oxford historian of modern history, is convinced that what Christians do in prayer is the most significant factor in the shaping of history—more significant than war and diplomacy, more significant than technology and art.—Eugene Peterson in Under the Unpredictable Plant*

7. Compare Jonah 2:7 with the verses from Psalms below. What similarities do you see?

Jonah 2:7 When my life was ebbing away, I called out to the LORD, and my prayer came to your holy temple.

Psalm 11:4 The LORD is in his holy temple; the LORD's throne is in heaven.

Psalm 65:4 How blessed is the one whom you choose, and allow to live in your palace courts. May we be satisfied with the good things of your house—your holy palace. (Note: The word for *temple* and *palace* are the same in Hebrew. Context determines how we translate.)

_____

_____

_____

8. Compare Jonah 2:8 with the verse from Psalms below. What similarities do you see?

Jonah 2:8 Those who worship worthless idols forfeit the mercy that could be theirs.

Psalm 31:6 I hate those who serve worthless idols, but I trust in the LORD.

_____

_____

_____

9. Compare Jonah 2:9 with the verses from Psalms below. What similarities do you see?

Jonah 2:9 But as for me, I promise to offer a sacrifice to you with a public declaration of praise; I will surely do what I have promised. Salvation belongs to the LORD!"

Psalm 3:8 The LORD delivers; you show favor to your people.

Psalm 116:14 I will fulfill my vows to the LORD before all his people.

Psalm 50:14 Present to God a thank-offering! Repay your vows to the sovereign One!

Psalm 50:23 "Whoever presents a thank-offering honors me. To whoever obeys my commands, I will reveal my power to deliver."

_____

_____

10. Because we're working with translation, it's sometimes difficult to see where the phrases are quite similar. Still, we can see parallel ideas. What conclusions might we draw about Jonah's interaction with Scripture and his prayer life from all of this?

_____

_____

11. Jonah appears to have had a solid knowledge of Scripture and God's ways. Why do you think such knowledge didn't keep him from running away?

_____

_____

_____

12. What are potential pitfalls of having a lot of spiritual knowledge? Is it bad to know a lot about God and his Word?

_____

_____

_____

FRIDAY: IN A TIGHT SPOT

1. Ask the Holy Spirit to grant you insight into the text; then read aloud Jonah's prayer:

> **1:17** The LORD sent a huge fish to swallow Jonah, and Jonah was in the stomach of the fish three days and three nights.

2:1 Jonah prayed to the LORD his God from the stomach of the fish

2:2 and said, "I called out to the LORD from my distress,
and he answered me;
from the belly of Sheol I cried out for help,
and you heard my prayer.

2:3 You threw me into the deep waters,
into the middle of the sea;
the ocean current engulfed me;
all the mighty waves you sent swept over me.

2:4 I thought I had been banished from your sight,
that I would never again see your holy temple!

2:5 Water engulfed me up to my neck;
the deep ocean surrounded me;
seaweed was wrapped around my head.

2:6 I went down to the very bottoms of the mountains;
the gates of the netherworld barred me in forever;
but you brought me up from the Pit, O LORD, my God.

2:7 When my life was ebbing away, I called out to the LORD,
and my prayer came to your holy temple.

2:8 Those who worship worthless idols forfeit the mercy that could be theirs.

2:9 But as for me, I promise to offer a sacrifice to you with a public declaration of praise;
I will surely do what I have promised.
Salvation belongs to the LORD!"

2:10 Then the LORD commanded the fish and it disgorged Jonah on dry land.

2. What do you find most interesting or unexpected in Jonah's prayer?

---

3. In this passage we see Jonah in prayer for the first time. Remarkably, this is not a cry of desperation but of praise for escape from physical death. Experts view Jonah's response to God in two completely different ways. Some see Jonah praising God despite his difficulties because God has given him a second chance. Others see Jonah in denial, praising when he should be lamenting and repenting. To them Jonah comes off as familiar with prayers used in worship at the Jerusalem temple—reciting the Scriptures—but missing the spirit behind them and misapplying them in his own situation. What do you think and why?

_____

_____

_____

- *From the belly of Sheol* (2:2). Jonah says he called to the Lord from the belly of Sheol. At this time in history, God's people did not have a fully developed view of the afterlife. Today we have much more of God's revelation to go on, such as the beautiful picture of heaven with no more night or pain or tears as seen in Revelation 21.

  The word *Sheol* refers to the invisible underworld beneath mountains and seas where people descended at death (Deut. 32:22; Job 26:6). It was considered a dark, gloomy place from which no one returned and a place from which the righteous were saved. Sometimes Sheol was personified as a ravenous monster.

  The King James translators often rendered this word "grave" or sometimes "pit." But it really means "the place where the dead abide." Its Greek equivalent—and the word chosen by the Septuagint team that translated Scripture from Hebrew to Greek—is *hades*. According to the *International Bible Encyclopedia*:

  > When life is ended, the dead are gathered in their tribes and families. Hence, the expression frequently occurring in the Pentateuch, 'to be gathered to one's people,' 'to go to one's fathers,' etc. (Gen 15:15; 25:8, 17; 49:33; Num 20:24, 28; 31:2; Deut 32:50; 34:5). It is figured as an under-world

(Isa 44:23; Ezek 26:20). . . . It is a 'land of forgetfulness,' where God's 'wonders' are unknown' (Psa 88:10–12). There is no remembrance or praise of God (Psa 6:5; 88:12; 115:17). In its darkness, stillness, powerlessness, lack of knowledge and inactivity, it is a true abode of death; hence, it is regarded by the living with shrinking, horror and dismay (Psa 39:13; Isa 38:17–19), though to the weary and troubled it may present the aspect of a welcome rest or sleep (Job 3:17–22).[5]

4. Jonah prayed, "From the belly of Sheol I cried out for help, and you heard my prayer" (2:2). Based on what we know of Sheol, what do you think Jonah was saying?

_____

_____

_____

5. The text says that the *sailors* tossed Jonah overboard as a last resort. Yet Jonah said to God, "*You* threw me into the deep waters, into the middle of the sea" (2:3, italics added). How do you reconcile the events as they happened with Jonah's prayer? That is, who threw Jonah into the sea and what does your answer say about God's ability to control human events?

_____

_____

_____

6. Reread Jonah 2:4–7. State in your own words what Jonah appears to be expressing here.

2:4 I thought I had been banished from your sight,
that I would never again see your holy temple!
2:5 Water engulfed me up to my neck;

[5]International Standard Bible Encyclopedia, CD-ROM, "Sheol."

the deep ocean surrounded me;
seaweed was wrapped around my head.
2:6 I went down to the very bottoms of the mountains;
the gates of the netherworld barred me in forever;
but you brought me up from the Pit, O LORD, my God.
2:7 When my life was ebbing away, I called out to the LORD,
and my prayer came to your holy temple.

---

7. Jonah called out to the Lord. What do you think is implied by the words "And my prayer came to your holy temple"? Isn't God everywhere?

- *Those who worship worthless idols forfeit the mercy that could be theirs* (2:8). The word for mercy on Jonah's lips is *hesed*. (It's pronounced with a hard *h* and rhymes with "BLESS-ed.") *Hesed* is an important word throughout the Old Testament. In fact, if you're going to memorize one Hebrew word in addition to *shalom* and *hallelujah*, it should probably be *hesed*. Why? Because God uses this very word to describe his own character (Ex. 34:6). It's the word Jonah will use later to describe God when he's ticked off that the Lord won't destroy the Ninevites. Note that Jonah seems happy to receive mercy here, but he's not too excited when God shows it to others later.

  Hesed seems to be the one word chosen above all others to summarize what God is like: full of loyal, committed, merciful, enduring, faithful, covenant-keeping love. An act of *hesed* is often demonstrated as covenant assistance shown to a vulnerable party, to one unable to help himself or herself. Wealthy Boaz shows *hesed* to hungry Ruth and Naomi. God shows *hesed* to his people. And Jonah is suggesting that idol worshipers can experience such loyal, covenant love from God if they so choose. Notice the strong missionary emphasis implied in this statement.

8. Jonah made a promise similar to that of the Phoenician sailors:

> **Jonah 2:9** But as for me, I promise to offer a sacrifice to you with a public declaration of praise; I will surely do what I have promised. Salvation belongs to the LORD!"

After God spared the sailors, the text says: "The men feared the LORD greatly, and earnestly vowed to offer lavish sacrifices to the LORD" (Jon. 1:16). Both the sailors and Jonah are spared and both respond with promises to sacrifice—an appropriate response. Have you or someone you love ever faced a near-death experience? If so, what was your response?

_____

_____

9. Do you think Jonah truly intended to praise God, or do you think his focus was more on contrasting himself with those who worshiped idols and coming out ahead? (There's no "right" answer here.)

_____

_____

10. Do you think we ever see Jonah totally obedient? Why or why not? What, in your opinion, is the high point of his faith in this book?

_____

_____

_____

11. **Bonus Question.** Imagine you are Jonah, and you realize you've totally messed up. Write out your prayer of repentance.

_____

_____

_____

SATURDAY: GRIPE IN THE SPIRIT

My husband and I spent a decade facing infertility, multiple pregnancy losses, and failed adoptions before we finally celebrated the arrival of our daughter. Ultimately doctors discovered that I have an immune system condition that causes my body to attack an embryo, but at the time we had no idea why we were enduring so much heartbreak.

After each pregnancy loss, I found myself drawn to the psalms. Lines such as, "How long, O LORD?" (6:3, NIV) and "My God, my God, why have you forsaken me?" (22:1, NIV) filled my prayers. While exploring how to offer these spiritual complaints, I discovered to my surprise that the prayer of lament is *the most common form* of psalm in the Bible. (We're in trouble a lot!) Pain is part of the human condition, and as it turns out, God inspired lots of angst-filled words for us to pray back to him. Sometimes we have trouble forming words to express ourselves, and to our delight we find God has given us some preformed examples as a guide.

I had once thought it might be unspiritual or faithless to ask God questions or to complain when I had so many blessings. But my journey through the psalms revealed otherwise. Once I learned to pray with the psalmists, I wrote some psalms of my own—like this one:

O Lord, not again.

How could you allow this again?

Once more the doctor has said our baby's gone, and I feel pain deeper than my own soul.

Our friends say, "Maybe you can have another," but why would you let me conceive this one if it wasn't going to live?

I want *this* child, Lord! How long must we keep going through this endless cycle of hope and despair? It feels so cruel.

I hate it and I don't understand it, but I have nowhere to go but to you.

Please help me to trust you.

Now, something notably absent in Jonah's prayer is any evidence of lament or repentance. And because the Book of Jonah is full of irony at every turn, it's possible we're to see in his prayer a touch of irony as well. Why didn't he express his fear? Why didn't he verbalize the trauma? Did he wonder how he'd ever get back to land alive? Did he regret trying to run from an omnipresent God? Did he care that he'd been a terrible testimony to some kind Phoenicians? If so, we see not a shred of evidence.

Calvin Miller, one of my favorite authors, has observed that "weeping is a sign of life." Keeping a stiff upper lip, pretending all is well, refusing to let others know of our brokenness—these are not signs of spiritual health. Wearing a spiritual facade is not a functional way to deal with life on a planet that writhes in pain like a woman in hard labor.

So be honest. Tell God how you feel. Cry when you need to. Sure, include praise; we have much to be thankful for. Still, be sure to tell the Lord about how it hurts and how you sin and need to forgive others who've sinned against you.

Jesus said we would have trouble in this world. But he also said he has overcome the world. Joy in the Christian life comes not because God has taken away our pain; it comes because even in the middle of it all, even in the terrible moment when you've miscarried your seventh baby and you suffer from a complete lack of trust, God is there. He is very near. And he cares.

Pray: *Almighty, omnipresent Father, thank you that I can never run and hide from you. If I cruise on the ocean, you're there. If I descend into a cave, you're there. If I fly at thirty thousand feet, you're there. Thank you that you have numbered every hair on my head and that your ways are always just. Help me to care for the desperate people around me who worship the idols of money and physical beauty and the constant thrill of a new romance. They need you. Help me to show them the way, not because I'm better, but because I myself have been rescued. Help me be honest with you about myself. Search me, O God, and know my heart. Try me and know my thoughts. See if there's any hurtful way in me and lead me in the everlasting way. In Jesus' name, amen.*

Memorize: "But as for me, I promise to offer a sacrifice to you with a public declaration of praise; I will surely do what I have promised. Salvation belongs to the LORD!" (Jon. 2:9).

WEEK 3 OF 4

The Shortest Sermon Ever Preached: Jonah 3

SUNDAY: JONAH'S TIMELESS MESSAGE

Scripture: The Lord is not slow concerning his promise, as some regard slowness, but is being patient toward you, because he does not wish for any to perish but for all to come to repentance (2 Pet. 3:9).

For today's time of reflection, join me on a journey through church history in looking at some of the early church fathers' insights into Jonah's story. Glean from their many wonderful reflections and observations. As we study the Bible, it's always good to connect with the community of faith, whether with present-time believers or with saints of the past through words left behind.

Gregory of Nazianzus (fourth century): "Let us show ourselves people of Nineveh, not of Sodom. Let us amend our wickedness, lest we be consumed with it. Let us listen to the preaching of Jonah, lest we be overwhelmed by fire and brimstone."—*On His Father's Silence, Oration 16.14.*

Augustine (fourth and fifth centuries): "A sovereign serves God one way as a man, another way as a king. He serves him as man by living according to faith. He serves him as king by exerting the necessary strength to sanction laws that command goodness and prohibit its opposite. It was thus that Ezekiel served him by destroying the groves and temples of idols and the high places that had been set up contrary to the commandments of God. Thus Josiah served him by performing similar acts. Thus the king of the Ninevites served him by compelling the whole city to appease the Lord."—*Letter 185.5.19.*

Maximus of Turin (fourth century): "The king conquered enemies with a display of valor. He conquered God, however, by humility. He is a wise king who, in order to save his people, owns himself a sinner rather than a king. He forgets that he is a king, fearing God the King of all. He does not bring to mind his own power but rather comes to possess the power of the Godhead. Marvelous! When he forgets that he is a king of men, he begins to be a king of righteousness."—*Commentary on Jonah*

John Chrysostom (fourth century): "Recall that Daniel, passionate man though he was, spent many days fasting. . . . The Ninevites too made use of the remedy of fasting and won from the Lord a reprieve. Animals as well as human beings were included in the fast, so that all living things would abstain from evil practices. This total response won the favor of the Lord of all."—*Homilies on Genesis 1.7.*

Clement of Rome (first century): "Let us look back over all the generations and learn that from generation to generation the Lord has given an opportunity of repentance to all who would return to him. Noah preached penance, and those who heeded were saved. Then Jonah announced destruction to the Ninevites and they repented of their sins, besought God in prayer and, estranged though they were from God, obtained salvation."—*1 Clement 7.*

MONDAY: JONAH FROM A DIFFERENT ANGLE

1. Pray for insight; then read the Book of Jonah again. (It's shorter than your average front-page newspaper story.) This time you'll read it in the *King James Version* so you can take a slightly different look at the text. Notice, as you read, the difference between what the text says about God's anger and what it records about Jonah's anger. In addi-

tion you will notice some italicized words. These are places where the Hebrew text does not include a word but does imply it.

Jonah 1

1 Now the word of the LORD came unto Jonah the son of Amittai, saying,

2 Arise, go to Nineveh, that great city, and cry against it; for their wickedness is come up before me. **3** But Jonah rose up to flee unto Tarshish from the presence of the LORD, and went down to Joppa; and he found a ship going to Tarshish: so he paid the fare thereof, and went down into it, to go with them unto Tarshish from the presence of the LORD.

4 But the LORD sent out a great wind into the sea, and there was a mighty tempest in the sea, so that the ship was like to be broken.

5 Then the mariners were afraid, and cried every man unto his god, and cast forth the wares that *were* in the ship into the sea, to lighten *it* of them. But Jonah was gone down into the sides of the ship; and he lay, and was fast asleep.

6 So the shipmaster came to him, and said unto him, What meanest thou, O sleeper? arise, call upon thy God, if so be that God will think upon us, that we perish not.

7 And they said every one to his fellow, Come, and let us cast lots, that we may know for whose cause this evil *is* upon us. So they cast lots, and the lot fell upon Jonah.

8 Then said they unto him, Tell us, we pray thee, for whose cause this evil *is* upon us; What *is* thine occupation? and whence comest thou? what *is* thy country? and of what people *art* thou?

9 And he said unto them, I *am* an Hebrew; and I fear the LORD, the God of heaven, which hath made the sea and the dry *land*.

10 Then were the men exceedingly afraid, and said unto him, Why hast thou done this? For the men knew that he fled from the presence of the LORD, because he had told them.

11 Then said they unto him, What shall we do unto thee, that the sea may be calm unto us? for the sea wrought, and was tempestuous.

12 And he said unto them, Take me up, and cast me forth into the sea; so shall the sea be calm unto you: for I know that for my sake this great tempest *is* upon you.

13 Nevertheless the men rowed hard to bring *it* to the land; but they could not: for the sea wrought, and was tempestuous against them.

14 Wherefore they cried unto the Lᴏʀᴅ, and said, We beseech thee, O Lᴏʀᴅ, we beseech thee, let us not perish for this man's life, and lay not upon us innocent blood: for thou, O Lᴏʀᴅ, hast done as it pleased thee.

15 So they took up Jonah, and cast him forth into the sea: and the sea ceased from her raging.

16 Then the men feared the Lᴏʀᴅ exceedingly, and offered a sacrifice unto the Lᴏʀᴅ, and made vows.

17 Now the Lᴏʀᴅ had prepared a great fish to swallow up Jonah. And Jonah was in the belly of the fish three days and three nights.

Jonah 2

1 Then Jonah prayed unto the Lᴏʀᴅ his God out of the fish's belly,

2 And said, I cried by reason of mine affliction unto the Lᴏʀᴅ, and he heard me; out of the belly of hell cried I, *and* thou heardest my voice.

3 For thou hadst cast me into the deep, in the midst of the seas; and the floods compassed me about: all thy billows and thy waves passed over me.

4 Then I said, I am cast out of thy sight; yet I will look again toward thy holy temple.

5 The waters compassed me about, *even* to the soul: the depth closed me round about, the weeds were wrapped about my head.

6 I went down to the bottoms of the mountains; the earth with her bars *was* about me for ever: yet hast thou brought up my life from corruption, O Lᴏʀᴅ my God.

7 When my soul fainted within me I remembered the Lᴏʀᴅ: and my prayer came in unto thee, into thine holy temple.

8 They that observe lying vanities forsake their own mercy.

9 But I will sacrifice unto thee with the voice of thanksgiving; I will pay *that* that I have vowed. Salvation *is* of the Lᴏʀᴅ.

10 And the Lᴏʀᴅ spake unto the fish, and it vomited out Jonah upon the dry *land*.

Jonah 3

1 And the word of the Lᴏʀᴅ came unto Jonah the second time, saying,

2 Arise, go unto Nineveh, that great city, and preach unto it the preaching that I bid thee.

3 So Jonah arose, and went unto Nineveh, according to the word of the LORD. Now Nineveh was an exceeding great city of three days' journey.

4 And Jonah began to enter into the city a day's journey, and he cried, and said, Yet forty days, and Nineveh shall be overthrown.

5 So the people of Nineveh believed God, and proclaimed a fast, and put on sackcloth, from the greatest of them even to the least of them.

6 For word came unto the king of Nineveh, and he arose from his throne, and he laid his robe from him, and covered *him* with sackcloth, and sat in ashes.

7 And he caused *it* to be proclaimed and published through Nineveh by the decree of the king and his nobles, saying, Let neither man nor beast, herd nor flock, taste any thing: let them not feed, nor drink water:

8 But let man and beast be covered with sackcloth, and cry mightily unto God: yea, let them turn every one from his evil way, and from the violence that *is* in their hands.

9 Who can tell *if* God will turn and repent, and turn away from his fierce anger, that we perish not?

10 And God saw their works, that they turned from their evil way; and God repented of the evil, that he had said that he would do unto them; and he did *it* not.

Jonah 4

1 But it displeased Jonah exceedingly, and he was very angry.

2 And he prayed unto the LORD, and said, I pray thee, O LORD, *was* not this my saying, when I was yet in my country? Therefore I fled before unto Tarshish: for I knew that thou *art* a gracious God, and merciful, slow to anger, and of great kindness, and repentest thee of the evil.

3 Therefore now, O LORD, take, I beseech thee, my life from me; for *it is* better for me to die than to live.

4 Then said the LORD, Doest thou well to be angry?

5 So Jonah went out of the city, and sat on the east side of the city, and there made him a booth, and sat under it in the shadow, till he might see what would become of the city.

6 And the LORD God prepared a gourd, and made *it* to come up over Jonah, that it might be a shadow over his head, to deliver him from his grief. So Jonah was exceeding glad of the gourd.

7 But God prepared a worm when the morning rose the next day, and it smote the gourd that it withered.

8 And it came to pass, when the sun did arise, that God prepared a vehement east wind; and the sun beat upon the head of Jonah, that he fainted, and wished in himself to die, and said, *It is* better for me to die than to live.

9 And God said to Jonah, Doest thou well to be angry for the gourd? And he said, I do well to be angry, *even* unto death.

10 Then said the LORD, Thou hast had pity on the gourd, for the which thou hast not laboured, neither madest it grow; which came up in a night, and perished in a night:

11 And should not I spare Nineveh, that great city, wherein are more than sixscore thousand persons that cannot discern between their right hand and their left hand; and *also* much cattle?

2. What stood out to you in this reading?

_____

_____

3. What did you notice about God's character?

_____

_____

_____

4. What did you notice about humanity?

_____

_____

_____

I called out to the LORD from my distress, and he answered me; from the belly of Sheol I cried out for help, and you heard my prayer. You threw me into the deep waters, into the middle of the sea; the ocean current engulfed me; all the mighty waves you sent swept over me. I thought I had been banished from your sight, that I would never again see your holy temple! Water engulfed me up to my neck; the deep ocean surrounded me; seaweed was wrapped around my head. I went down to the very bottoms of the mountains; the gates of the netherworld barred me in forever; but you brought me up from the Pit, O LORD, my God. When my life was ebbing away, I called out to the LORD, and my prayer came to your holy temple. Those who worship worthless idols forfeit the mercy that could be theirs. But as for me, I promise to offer a sacrifice to you with a public declaration of praise; I will surely do what I have promised. Salvation belongs to the LORD! (Jon 2:2–9).

5. Perhaps you've just survived a "storm." If so, offer Jonah's comilation of psalm phrases to God as an act of worship.

TUESDAY: JONAH GETS A DO-OVER

1. The focus of our study this week is Jonah 3. While Jonah 3 is a chapter in the Bible, it's not like a book chapter in length; it's actually only about as long as two average paragraphs. Pray for insight; then read it again:

Jonah 3:1 The LORD said to Jonah a second time, **3:2** "Go immediately to Nineveh, that large city, and proclaim to it the message that I tell you." **3:3** So Jonah went immediately to Nineveh, as the LORD had said. (Now Nineveh was an enormous city—it required three days to walk through it!) **3:4** When Jonah began to enter the city one day's walk, he announced, "At the end of forty days, Nineveh will be overthrown!"

3:5 The people of Nineveh believed in God, and they declared a fast and put on sackcloth, from the greatest to the least of them. **3:6** When the news reached the king of Nineveh, he got up from his throne, took off his royal robe, put on sackcloth, and sat on ashes. **3:7** He issued a proclamation and said, "In Nineveh, by the decree of the king and his nobles: No human or animal, cattle or sheep, is to taste anything; they must not eat and they must not drink water. **3:8** Every person and animal must put on sackcloth and must cry earnestly to God, and everyone must turn from their evil way of living and from the violence that they do. **3:9** Who knows? Perhaps God might be willing to change his mind and relent and turn from his fierce anger so that we might not die." **3:10** When God saw their actions—they turned from their evil way of living!—God relented concerning the judgment he had threatened them with and he did not destroy them.

2. Circle the word *immediately* in verses 2 and 3 in the previous passage. What was different in Jonah's response to God this time around?

_____

_____

_____

3. We see many parallels between Jonah 1 and 3. Compare them.

The Commission
Where was Jonah sent (Jonah 1:1–2)?

_____

Where was Jonah sent (Jonah 3:1–2)?

_____

Imminent Doom
Who was threatened with destruction in Jonah 1:4–13?

_____

Who was threatened with destruction in Jonah 3:4–7?

_____

Submitting to God
Who cried to Yahweh in 1:14?

_____

Whom may we assume cried to Yahweh in 3:8–9?

_____

Mercy Demonstrated
Who was saved from destruction in 1:15?

_____

Who was saved from destruction in 3:10?

_____

4. Often in Scripture, especially in the book of Judges, we see a pattern: Disobedience →Divine Discipline → Dedication → Deliverance. Describe how this pattern appears in the Book of Jonah.

_____

_____

_____

_____

5. What does this pattern reveal about God?

_____

_____

_____

_____

6. God recommissioned Jonah (3:1–2). Record a time when God gave you a second chance. How did you feel?

_____

_____

_____

7. Based on what you've studied so far, how would you answer those who say that the God of the Old Testament is mean and vindictive?

_____

_____

_____

WEDNESDAY: THE MESSAGE

1. Pray for insight; then read Jonah 3:1–4:

> **Jonah 3:1** The LORD said to Jonah a second time, **3:2** "Go immediately to Nineveh, that large city, and proclaim to it the message that I tell you." **3:3** So Jonah went immediately to Nineveh, as the LORD had said. (Now Nineveh was an enormous city—it required three days to walk through it!) **3:4** When Jonah began to enter the city one day's walk, he announced, "At the end of forty days, Nineveh will be overthrown!"

- *Nineveh was an enormous city* (3:3). The author describes Nineveh literally as "a great city to Elohim." *Great* here doesn't mean "wonderful" like a "great musician"; it refers to size. The phrase *great to God (Elohim)* is a Hebrew idiom for "very important."
- *It required three days to walk through it!* (3:3). Some have understood this statement about the city's size to refer to its diameter. That would make Nineveh about a fifty-mile walk from one end to the other. This description fails to line up with archeological findings, which measure the city's circumference

at about seven miles. Nor does a fifty-mile diameter line up with good sense. While Nineveh was large, it wasn't *that* large! This alone makes some conclude the book *has* to be an allegory. Yet others see "three days to walk through" as having in view the greater Nineveh metropolis rather than the walled city alone. I live in the Dallas/Fort Worth metroplex, and even though I actually live in Mesquite, Texas, I usually say I'm from Dallas. Most people who live outside Dallas proper but within the Dallas metro area say the same thing. This being the case, for Jonah to effectively evangelize the entire Nineveh metropolis would have required a three-day preaching tour.

2. Jonah preached the shortest sermon in the Bible (3:4). He didn't even preface his words with "Thus says the Lord." What was his message?

_____

_____

_____

It's possible that Jonah said much more than the words quoted here but the author didn't record it all because transcribing was not the author's style. It's also possible Jonah didn't speak the language and memorized only the necessary words. Some, however, see in Jonah's sermon his continuing reluctance to proclaim God's message as he stated the absolute minimum required (this is *legalism*). This explanation would fit with the irony constantly emphasized throughout the book.

3. **Optional:** Jonah referred to "forty days." Does this bring to mind another Bible story in which judgment lasted forty days? Do you see any parallels between the stories?

_____

_____

_____

4. Imagine what the fish's stomach acid would have done to Jonah's hair and pigment. How would he have looked when he arrived in Nineveh?

_____

_____

_____

_____

5. Remember back in week 1 when we considered that Nineveh's native name and worship were probably connected to fish? Fish are plentiful in the Tigris at Mosul, the modern town across the river from ancient Nineveh, and the presence of fish at the ancient site may have influenced the Babylonian settlers to erect a temple to Ishtar or Nina. Bearing in mind these cultural factors, what might Nineveh's fish-worshiping citizens have thought when they heard of Jonah coming "by fish," arriving bald and bleached from fish-stomach acid to bring a message from the God who made heaven, earth, and sea?

_____

_____

_____

_____

6. **Bonus Question:** Imagine Jonah's story as a drama. Who would you cast as Jonah? As the king of Nineveh? The captain of the sailors? The voice of God? The plant? Would you give the drama a modern or ancient setting? Would you actually clothe all the animals in sackcloth? (Nineveh had many gods relating to animals, so the fact that they made their animals fast may indicate their subjection to the true God.) If you're a creative type, consider making a *Playbill* that describes each character, scene, and actor and the credits for the persons acting the parts. (For formatting ideas, go to www.playbill.com.)

1. Pray for insight; then read Jonah 3:4–9:

> **3:4** When Jonah began to enter the city one day's walk, he announced, "At the end of forty days, Nineveh will be overthrown!" **3:5** The people of Nineveh believed in God, and they declared a fast and put on sackcloth, from the greatest to the least of them. **3:6** When the news reached the king of Nineveh, he got up from his throne, took off his royal robe, put on sackcloth, and sat on ashes. **3:7** He issued a proclamation and said, "In Nineveh, by the decree of the king and his nobles: No human or animal, cattle or sheep, is to taste anything; they must not eat and they must not drink water. **3:8** Every person and animal must put on sackcloth and must cry earnestly to God, and everyone must turn from their evil way of living and from the violence that they do. **3:9** Who knows? Perhaps God might be willing to change his mind and relent and turn from his fierce anger so that we might not die."

2. According to 3:4–5, when did the people repent?

_____

_____

_____

3. What did the Ninevites do when they heard Jonah's message (3:5)?

_____

_____

_____

• *They believed in God* (3:5). Notice that the word for God here (as well as vv. 8–9) is not *Yahweh*, which has been used up to this point. Rather, we find the more generic *Elohim* (God). The Ninevites feared God enough to turn from evil and ask for help, similar to how Americans filed into churches after 9/11. Yet we should avoid making more out of the Ninevites' actions than the text does, in the same way we should avoid assuming millions in the U.S. trusted Christ as their Savior in 2001. About one hundred years after the events described in Jonah, Nineveh *was* destroyed. Yet notice that even the rather surface-level turning from evil toward God described in Jonah 3:5 caused the Lord to relent. How gracious he is! And how quick we should be to affirm any movement toward him.

- *They declared a fast* (3:5). Sometimes people fast so they can give the money they would have spent on food to the poor. In the Book of Jonah, the Ninevites fasted out of a humble desire to stop God from destroying them. They demonstrated their reverence, their seriousness about changing their ways, and their fervent hope that God would relent about the coming judgment. Such practices are not only for those who have committed the kinds of evil and violence that the Assyrians practiced; James admonishes believers to mourn and weep (4:9).

If we draw our understanding of God only from what we hear on television, we might have a high view of God's love but a low view of his holiness. The Book of Jonah is about God's mercy, but notice that God's decision not to destroy the Ninevites follows their humility in response to his prophet's message of judgment.

The Lord Jesus taught about fasting, as recorded in Matthew 6:16–18. He said, "When you fast, do not look sullen like the hypocrites, for they make their faces unattractive so that people will see them fasting. I tell you the truth, they have their reward. When you fast, put oil on your head and wash your face, so that it will not be obvious to others when you are fasting, but only to your Father who is in secret. And your Father, who sees in secret, will reward you." Notice that the first word here is *when*, not *if*. In many churches today the topic of fasting never arises. Many spiritual leaders no longer teach about it because they associate such practices with legalism. But it doesn't have to be that way, any more than giving to the needy or praying are the activities of legalists. (Jesus said to do these in secret too.) Fasting is one way to demonstrate our humility toward God and our focus on spiritual food.

4. Plan to fast at least one meal in the next week if you have no medical reason to keep you from doing so. Each time you feel a wave of

hunger, allow the pangs to remind you to worship God in his holiness. What meal(s) on what day will you fast? How can you make fasting part of your routine?

_____

_____

_____

_____

- *And put on sackcloth* (3:6). The Bible records more than forty-five instances in which wearing sackcloth—a rough garment of goat's hair—over the naked body was a symbol of humility, grief, repentance, helplessness, and/or despair. Here's a brief sampling of references (emphasis added):

  David looked up and saw the Lord's messenger standing between the earth and sky with his sword drawn and in his hand stretched over Jerusalem. David and the leaders, *covered with sackcloth*, threw themselves down with their faces to the ground (1 Chron. 21:16).

  On the twenty-fourth day of this same month the Israelites assembled; they were *fasting and wearing sackcloth*, their heads covered with dust (Neh. 9:1).

  Now when Mordecai became aware of all that had been done, he tore his garments and *put on sackcloth and ashes*. He went out into the city, crying out in a loud and bitter voice (Esther 4:1).

  Then you turned my lament into dancing, you removed my *sackcloth* and covered me with joy (Ps. 30:11).

  When they were sick, *I wore sackcloth and refrained from eating food* (Ps. 35:13).

  So *put on sackcloth*. Mourn and wail, saying, "The fierce anger of the LORD has not turned away from us" (Jer. 4:8).

  Woe to you, Chorazin! Woe to you, Bethsaida! If the miracles done in you had been done in Tyre and Sidon, they would have *repented long ago in sackcloth and ashes* (Matt. 11:21).

5. How did Nineveh's king respond to Jonah's message (3:6)?

_____

_____

_____

6. What actions did the king's edict require of his subjects (3:7–9)?

_____

_____

_____

_____

7. According to this king, what sins did his nation need to turn away from (3:8)?

_____

_____

_____

8. Why did the king prescribe the measures laid out in the edict (3:9)?

_____

_____

_____

9. Step back a moment and consider the original audience for Jonah's story. This narrative was initially written to Israel to remind her to care about her neighbors. Bear in mind that the king reigning in Israel dur-

ing Jonah's lifetime did "evil in the sight of the Lord." Imagine Israel's citizens hearing this story. How do the actions of Nineveh's king compare with what we know of those of Israel's many wicked kings? What about the actions of Nineveh's citizens?

_____

_____

_____

10. Pray for your nation that God would bring both leaders and citizens to repentance—starting with you.

11. Repentance means more than feeling remorse or apologizing. It begins with confession to God and (in some cases) to the humans wronged, and it involves making a complete turn in one's actions and attitudes. Spend time confessing your sins to God and to others with whom you need to make amends. Ask the Spirit to grant you the grace to make a complete turn in your hurtful ways.

12. **Bonus Question:** After King David committed adultery with Bathsheba, he arranged the death of her loyal husband. One might think God could never forgive such offenses, and indeed, David's actions grieved the Spirit. Yet David eventually repented, and tradition records that David wrote Psalm 32 and Psalm 51 as his response to God's lavish grace. Having asked forgiveness from your own sins, meditate on these beautiful Scriptures:

Psalm 32

32:1 How blessed is the one whose rebellious acts are forgiven,
whose sin is pardoned!
32:2 How blessed is the one whose wrongdoing the Lord does not punish,
in whose spirit there is no deceit.
32:3 When I refused to confess my sin,
my whole body wasted away,
while I groaned in pain all day long.

32:4 For day and night you tormented me;

you tried to destroy me in the intense heat of summer. (Selah)

32:5 Then I confessed my sin;

I no longer covered up my wrongdoing.

I said, "I will confess my rebellious acts to the Lord."

And then you forgave my sins. (Selah)

32:6 For this reason every one of your faithful followers should pray to you

while there is a window of opportunity.

Certainly when the surging water rises,

it will not reach them.

32:7 You are my hiding place;

you protect me from distress.

You surround me with shouts of joy from those celebrating deliverance. (Selah)

32:8 I will instruct and teach you about how you should live.

I will advise you as I look you in the eye.

32:9 Do not be like an unintelligent horse or mule,

which will not obey you

unless they are controlled by a bridle and bit.

32:10 An evil person suffers much pain,

but the Lord's faithfulness overwhelms the one who trusts in him.

32:11 Rejoice in the Lord and be happy, you who are godly!

Shout for joy, all you who are morally upright!

Psalm 51

51:1 Have mercy on me, O God, because of your loyal love!

Because of your great compassion, wipe away my rebellious acts!

51:2 Wash away my wrongdoing!

Cleanse me of my sin!

51:3 For I am aware of my rebellious acts;

I am forever conscious of my sin.

51:4 Against you – you above all – I have sinned;

I have done what is evil in your sight.

So you are just when you confront me;
you are right when you condemn me.

51:5 Look, I was guilty of sin from birth,
a sinner the moment my mother conceived me.

51:6 Look, you desire integrity in the inner man;
you want me to possess wisdom.

51:7 Sprinkle me with water and I will be pure;
wash me and I will be whiter than snow.

51:8 Grant me the ultimate joy of being forgiven!
May the bones you crushed rejoice!

51:9 Hide your face from my sins!
Wipe away all my guilt!

51:10 Create for me a pure heart, O God!
Renew a resolute spirit within me!

51:11 Do not reject me!
Do not take your Holy Spirit away from me!

51:12 Let me again experience the joy of your deliverance!
Sustain me by giving me the desire to obey!

51:13 Then I will teach rebels your merciful ways,
and sinners will turn to you.

51:14 Rescue me from the guilt of murder, O God, the God who delivers me!

Then my tongue will shout for joy because of your deliverance.

51:15 O Lord, give me the words!
Then my mouth will praise you.

51:16 Certainly you do not want a sacrifice, or else I would offer it;
you do not desire a burnt sacrifice.

51:17 The sacrifices God desires are a humble spirit –
O God, a humble and repentant heart you will not reject.

51:18 Because you favor Zion, do what is good for her!
Fortify the walls of Jerusalem!

51:19 Then you will accept the proper sacrifices, burnt sacrifices and whole offerings;
then bulls will be sacrificed on your altar.

Notice the words of hope in Psalm 51:13. The psalmist prays that God will use him to teach others to avoid the same pitfalls. He assumes that a truly repentant, reformed believer belongs not "on the shelf," retired from meaningful service, but rather "in the trenches," allowing God to make beauty from ashes.

FRIDAY: REPENTING AND RELENTING

1. In today's reading we see God's response to the Ninevites' repentance:

> **Jonah 3:10** When God saw their actions—they turned from their evil way of living!—God relented concerning the judgment he had threatened them with and he did not destroy them.

You knew he was going to do that, didn't you?

God is steadfast and unchanging, yet he relented and did not destroy Nineveh. Can you explain this seeming contradiction?
[insert lines for writing]

_____

_____

_____

2. Pray for God to grant you help in understanding; then read Romans 9:14–21:

> **Romans 9:14** What shall we say then? Is there injustice with God? Absolutely not! **9:15** For he says to Moses: "I will have mercy on whom I have mercy, and I will have compassion on whom I have compassion." **9:16** So then, it does not depend on human desire or exertion, but on God who shows mercy. **9:17** For the scripture says to Pharaoh: "For this very purpose I have raised you up, that I may demonstrate my power in you, and that my name may be proclaimed in all the earth." **9:18** So then, God has mercy on whom he chooses to have mercy, and he hardens whom he chooses to harden.
>
> **9:19** You will say to me then, "Why does he still find fault? For who has ever resisted his will?" **9:20** But who indeed are you – a

mere human being – to talk back to God? Does what is molded say to the molder, "Why have you made me like this?" **9:21** Has the potter no right to make from the same lump of clay one vessel for special use and another for ordinary use? **9:22** But what if God, willing to demonstrate his wrath and to make known his power, has endured with much patience the objects of wrath prepared for destruction? **9:23** And what if he is willing to make known the wealth of his glory on the objects of mercy that he has prepared beforehand for glory – **9:24** even us, whom he has called, not only from the Jews but also from the Gentiles?

What does this passage tell you about God's character when it comes to wrath and mercy?

_____

_____

_____

3. Ask for insight; then read Genesis 6:5–7:

Genesis 6:5 But the LORD saw that the wickedness of humankind had become great on the earth. Every inclination of the thoughts of their minds was only evil all the time. **6:6** The LORD regretted that he had made humankind on the earth, and he was highly offended. **6:7** So the LORD said, "I will wipe humankind, whom I have created, from the face of the earth—everything from humankind to animals, including creatures that move on the ground and birds of the air, for I regret that I have made them." **6:8** But Noah found favor in the sight of the Lord.

What does this story tell you about God's wrath and mercy?

_____

_____

_____

_____

4. Now read Exodus 32:8–14:

Exodus 32:8 They have quickly turned aside from the way that I commanded them – they have made for themselves a molten calf and have bowed down to it and sacrificed to it and said, 'These are your gods, O Israel, which brought you up from the land of Egypt.'"

32:9 Then the LORD said to Moses: "I have seen this people. Look what a stiff-necked people they are! **32:10** So now, leave me alone so that my anger can burn against them and I can destroy them, and I will make from you a great nation."

32:11 But Moses sought the favor of the LORD his God and said, "O LORD, why does your anger burn against your people, whom you have brought out from the land of Egypt with great power and with a mighty hand? **32:12** Why should the Egyptians say, 'For evil he led them out to kill them in the mountains and to destroy them from the face of the earth'? Turn from your burning anger, and relent of this evil against your people. **32:13** Remember Abraham, Isaac, and Israel your servants, to whom you swore by yourself and told them, 'I will multiply your descendants like the stars of heaven, and all this land that I have spoken about I will give to your descendants, and they will inherit it forever.'" **32:14** Then the LORD relented over the evil that he had said he would do to his people.

What in this story made God angry (32:8–9)?

_____

_____

_____

_____

5. What does the text suggest for why he relented (32:11–13)?

_____

_____

_____

_____

6. In the Exodus passage, what difference did it make for a righteous person to plead with God?

_____

_____

_____

7. Who needs your prayers for God's mercy? Spend time praying for yourself and others now.

8. God calls every Christian to tell others about their spiritual need, because he wants to show mercy, not wrath. A place to start is by sharing our own testimony of faith. Complete this simple outline about your conversion experience:
What I was like before Christ:

_____

_____

_____

How I heard about Christ and trusted in Him for salvation:

_____

_____

_____

What has changed since then:

_____

_____

_____

With whom will you share your story this week? Begin praying about that encounter.

9. Once you've fasted, write down any thoughts or observations.

_____

_____

_____

SATURDAY: PARENTING GOD'S WAY

When our daughter was a preteen, my husband and I developed a growing appreciation for how we should view threats from God about impending judgment. At parenting workshops we'd hear, "Don't make a threat and then fail to follow through. Once you make a rule, you can't change your mind. That's like lying. Your kids won't trust your word if you do that." Now for the most part, that was excellent advice. Yet sometimes, on *really* rare occasions, such advice got in the way of mercy and compassion—that is, it got in the way of good parenting.

Here's an example. We might say something to our daughter like, "Since you didn't clean your room like we told you to do, you can't go to Six Flags this weekend." On rare occasions—very rare, as I said—one of us would make such a statement only to be later guided by a preteen hand ("Close your eyes, Mom—it's a surprise!") and ushered into a clean room. And we might also then be led to the living room to find it vacuumed, and to the kitchen, where the dirty dishes had been washed. Then a child with big, round eyes would plead, "I know you warned me, but please, please, give me another chance. I'll go without TV for a week and pay my way out of my own allowance. I've had my heart set on this for a month, and I promised (insert name of kid who rarely attends church) that I'd be there!"

In a scenario like this, somehow saying, "I meant what I said" seemed just, but not merciful. More like rigid.

Of course, as I mentioned, such a response on the part of said child was extremely rare (maybe I dreamed it?), but that's all the more reason that a so-called parenting flip-flop is in order—as in, reinforce such unusual behavior!

I was thinking about all of this when I edited a story based on David and Bathsheba and I reread God's statement that the baby would die. David, the man after God's own heart, didn't interpret God's word as final until the baby actually passed away. That's because David knew God well enough to realize that sometimes a statement predicting doom is really a warning, not a decree.

Author Eugene Peterson has noted that the very thing that hacked off Jonah was that he was a literalist when it came to prophecy. Jonah *knew* better than to take God's word as final when there was room for mercy. Jonah knew that if God sends a warning, there's hope. If God wanted to obliterate the Ninevites, Jonah knew he would have done so without saying anything about it ahead of time. And that's what upset the rebel prophet!

Anytime we find a prediction of doom, there is an unstated glimmer of hope that if judgment hasn't already happened, God may relent. It may all depend on repentance.

Sometimes God follows through anyway, so relenting is not guaranteed. We must never presume upon God's grace. David's story—in which the baby ultimately dies—again comes to mind, and Sodom, where God did not find enough faithful people to hold back. Still, in Nineveh God is convinced the people need saving and their humility is worth rewarding.

If you have trusted in the finished work of Jesus Christ on the cross, you have been the recipient of such an about-face. If you haven't, what's stopping you? Do you still have areas of unconfessed sin? Of willful disobedience? Change your mind before it's too late!

Also, for whom should you be asking God to show grace, to relent in the face of deserved judgment? With whom can you share about God's *hesed*?

Pray: *Heavenly Father, thank you for your grace! You poured out your favor on me, even when I deserved punishment. You sent your Son to shed his own innocent blood so that I, a sinner, could escape your holy consequences. May I never get over your goodness to me! Use me, please, to tell others of your greatness, your patience, your lovingkindness. Change my heart to make it like yours, full of grace and mercy and longsuffering. Use me to spread the good news. In the name of your Son, amen.*

Memorize: When God saw their actions—they turned from their evil way of living!—God relented concerning the judgment he had threatened them with and he did not destroy them (Jon. 3:10).

Gracious God, Pouting Prophet: Jonah 4

SUNDAY: EXCESSIVE KINDNESS

Scripture: The Lord said, "You were upset about this little plant, something for which you have not worked nor did you do anything to make it grow. It grew up overnight and died the next day. Should I not be even more concerned about Nineveh, this enormous city? There are more than one hundred twenty thousand people in it who do not know right from wrong, as well as many animals!" (Jon. 4:10–11).

There's something about a furry, vulnerable creature that whispers to us of a greater world. Such creations help us understand what it's like to receive unconditional love—or at least acceptance, if the creature's a cat! (We have two such creatures.) Still, even an unaffectionate feline will brush against the leg, however briefly, of someone that another human might not dare to touch.

In the aftermath of Hurricane Katrina, I listened to horrific tales coming out of New Orleans. I recall one particularly sad story about a live dog wrapped in an electric cord in a tree, dying of electrocution. A cameraman watched helplessly, unable to get to the dog or even attempt a rescue. That dog was some family's loved canine, their pet. Heartbreaking!

If the loss of an animal can be this heart wrenching, how much more the loss of *human* life?

Such a perspective on life's value is exactly what God is getting at when he questioned the suicidal runaway prophet about his whining. After Jonah preached his get-right-or-get-left message to his Iraqi enemies, he parked on a hillside under some shade to watch God deliver some shock and awe.

But the people repented, so the Lord relented. And Jonah whooped, hollered, danced, even bragged about his part in the biggest revival in history, right?

Wrong.

He went postal, irate that God had the audacity to spare his enemies! Jonah was so full of rage, in fact, that he told the Lord that he was "angry unto death."

In responding this way, Jonah revealed his low, low view of human life, both his own and that of his enemies. But he did something else too—he demonstrated that he prized something far less important, a silly little gourd that provided shade for a few hours. That gourd withered, thanks to a God-sent bug. And Jonah, the prophet with a great double standard, cried about his sunburned head—while wishing God would fry a city full of Iraqis!

So God asked a question. To paraphrase, he said, "Jonah, you've been concerned about this vine, though you did not tend it or make it grow. It sprang up overnight and died overnight. But Nineveh has more than a hundred and twenty thousand people that I created and tended for years. Many of the people don't even know their right hand from their left—not to mention the animals. Shouldn't I be concerned about them? If you're not going to care for the grown-ups, Jonah, can't you at least have some compassion for the children—and the critters? And now that you finally care about something, how is it that all you care about is a plant?"

We are left wondering if Jonah will ever get it. Frankly, we doubt he will.

Now, what is it that made Jonah so angry with God?

Grace. Jonah knew that the God of the Old Testament is a gracious God whose only unreasonable quality is his excessive kindness extended to the worst of sinners.

This reminds me of another story about someone who couldn't

stand the thought of grace—the older brother in the parable of the prodigal son. Consider how that story ends, with the audience wondering whether that brother would humble himself and welcome the repentant sinner.

In both stories we see how deeply self-righteousness offends God. Why? Because anyone who considers someone else to be undeserving of grace is living a huge double standard. None of us is righteous in our own strength. *All* have sinned and keep on falling short of God's glory (Rom. 3:23). All of us stand in need of grace.

My friend Celestin, from Rwanda, experienced the murder of six of his family members. Some years later, when Celestin was performing a baptism service in the river, a man approached—and that man was wearing the shirt of Celestin's dead brother. To make matters worse, the man wanted Celestin to baptize him! When Celestin asked where he got the shirt, it was revealed that this man's brother had killed Celestin's brother. Tempted to dunk this man and hold him under, Celestin prayed, and Jesus Christ reminded him that nails had been pounded into his hands and feet for Celestin. Today the two men serve as partners in ministry, testifying to the astounding power of God to change hearts.

God calls us to love our enemies not because they're lovable, but because we were once God's enemies too. Our sins nailed the Son of God to a cross. For this reason we can never look down on others for what they've done. We were once in their shoes.

Who in your life needs you to demonstrate rather than resent God's grace?

MONDAY: THE PLANT LOVER

1. Pray for insight; then read our text for the week to see Jonah's response to the greatest revival in history. Jonah should be excited, right?

> **Jonah 3:10** When God saw their actions—they turned from their evil way of living!—God relented concerning the judgment he had threatened them with and he did not destroy them.
>
> **4:1** This displeased Jonah terribly and he became very angry.
> **4:2** He prayed to the LORD and said, "Oh, LORD, this is just what I thought would happen when I was in my own country. This is what I tried to prevent by attempting to escape to Tarshish!—because I

knew that you are gracious and compassionate, slow to anger and abounding in mercy, and one who relents concerning threatened judgment. **4:3** So now, LORD, kill me instead, because I would rather die than live!" **4:4** The LORD said, "Are you really so very angry?"

4:5 Jonah left the city and sat down east of it. He made a shelter for himself there and sat down under it in the shade to see what would happen to the city. **4:6** The LORD God appointed a little plant and caused it to grow up over Jonah to be a shade over his head to rescue him from his misery. Now Jonah was very delighted about the little plant.

4:7 So God sent a worm at dawn the next day, and it attacked the little plant so that it dried up. **4:8** When the sun began to shine, God sent a hot east wind. So the sun beat down on Jonah's head, and he grew faint. So he despaired of life, and said, "I would rather die than live!" **4:9** God said to Jonah, "Are you really so very angry about the little plant?" And he said, "I am as angry as I could possibly be!" **4:10** The LORD said, "You were upset about this little plant, something for which you have not worked nor did you do anything to make it grow. It grew up overnight and died the next day. **4:11** Should I not be even more concerned about Nineveh, this enormous city? There are more than one hundred twenty thousand people in it who do not know right from wrong, as well as many animals!"

As mentioned, in Jonah 4 we see the greatest recorded revival in the history of humanity. Yet Jonah feels only suicidal rage. As one Hebrew scholar expressed Jonah's point of view, "God is too good and that is too bad!"[6]

2. What questions appear in this passage?

_____

_____

_____

_____

[6]Class notes, Dr. Ronald B. Allen, Dallas Theological Seminary.

3. What do the questions reveal about the character of God?

_____

_____

_____

Texas pastor Bob Deffinbaugh tells this story about his stubborn, fearless cat:

> We once had a Siamese cat that didn't have the sense to back away from danger. Our landlord kept a burro named HeHaw in a pasture next to our house. HeHaw was pregnant, which made her even more cantankerous than ever. One day when we went over to the fence to check on HeHaw, our cat followed. Worse yet, the cat began to stalk the burro. The burro looked threateningly at the cat, but neither [my wife] nor I had any intention of getting around the backside of that burrow to retrieve our cat, so we kept hoping that it would have enough sense to know better than to antagonize that beast. The inevitable happened—the cat transgressed the boundary established by the burro. With one swift kick, the cat was launched into an orbit that sent it flying, landing a fair distance away. He got up shaking his head, having learned that burros are not impressed with cats, no matter how determined and fearless they might be.

Pastor Deffinbaugh draws a parallel between his cat's stubbornness and Jonah's:

> When I read the third and fourth chapters of the Book of Jonah, I get that same feeling that I had when I observed our cat stalking HeHaw. Jonah, like our cat, is stubbornly attacking God in chapter 4. He will seriously overstep his boundaries. As we read the chapter we just know that Jonah is going to get a proverbial "kick in the head" from God. And we will not be able to work up much sympathy for him if and when this happens.
>
> Strangely enough, Jonah is not kicked in the head, even though he deserves it. The book ends with a rebuke which lingers in mid-air, leaving the reader with a most uneasy feel-

ing. The book does not leave us with a warm fuzzy feeling, like we might wish it did. The book did not begin with a "Once upon a time . . ." Neither does it end with a "happily ever after."[7]

TUESDAY: FOILED AGAIN

1. In today's study we'll contrast Jonah's heart with God's. Pray for insight; then read Jonah 4:1–4, looking specifically at how different Jonah and God are:

> **Jonah 4:1** "[The fact that God relented] displeased Jonah terribly and he became very angry. **4:2** He prayed to the LORD and said, "Oh, LORD, this is just what I thought would happen when I was in my own country. This is what I tried to prevent by attempting to escape to Tarshish!—because I knew that you are gracious and compassionate, slow to anger and abounding in mercy, and one who relents concerning threatened judgment. **4:3** So now, LORD, kill me instead, because I would rather die than live!" **4:4** The LORD said, "Are you really so very angry?"

2. Jonah is a foil for God. That is, the prophet provides a black-velvet backdrop against which we can better see the diamonds of God's char-

---

[7]Dr. Deffinbaugh's notes on the Book of Jonah can be found at www.bible.org.

acter. What differences do you see between God's character and Jonah's? Who should have been the angry one in this story?

_____

_____

_____

3. Jonah was exceedingly angry and argued with God (4:1). In Acts 9:10–17, we read about another person who argued with God:

> **Acts 9:10** Now there was a disciple in Damascus named Ananias. The Lord said to him in a vision, "Ananias," and he replied, "Here I am, Lord." **9:11** Then the Lord told him, "Get up and go to the street called 'Straight,' and at Judas' house look for a man from Tarsus named Saul. For he is praying, **9:12** and he has seen in a vision a man named Ananias come in and place his hands on him so that he may see again." **9:13** But Ananias replied, "Lord, I have heard from many people about this man, how much harm he has done to your saints in Jerusalem, **9:14** and here he has authority from the chief priests to imprison all who call on your name!" **9:15** But the Lord said to him, "Go, because this man is my chosen instrument to carry my name before Gentiles and kings and the people of Israel. **9:16** For I will show him how much he must suffer for the sake of my name." **9:17** So Ananias departed and entered the house, placed his hands on Saul and said, "Brother Saul, the Lord Jesus, who appeared to you on the road as you came here, has sent me so that you may see again and be filled with the Holy Spirit."

What parallels and contrasts do you see in Jonah's and Ananias's experiences and responses?

Parallels

_____

_____

_____

Contrasts

_____

_____

_____

4. List the aspects of God's nature with which Jonah was quite familiar (4:2).

_____

_____

_____

5. Describe Jonah's relationship with God. That is, how well would you say Jonah knew him?

_____

_____

_____

Explain why you answered as you did.

_____

_____

_____

6. Assuming Jonah's description of God is accurate (it is), what kind of relationship do you think God wanted to have with Jonah? Do you think the Lord was satisfied once Jonah had finally done as he'd been told? Why or why not?

_____

_____

_____

7. Describe your own view of God and your relationship with him. Are you satisfied? Do you think God is? Why or why not?

_____

_____

_____

WEDNESDAY: DEATH WISH

1. Pray for insight; then reread Jonah 4:1–11. Circle every occurrence of the word *anger*.

Jonah 4:1 This displeased Jonah terribly and he became very angry. **4:2** He prayed to the LORD and said, "Oh, LORD, this is just what I thought would happen when I was in my own country. This is what I tried to prevent by attempting to escape to Tarshish!—because I knew that you are gracious and compassionate, slow to anger and abounding in mercy, and one who relents concerning threatened judgment. **4:3** So now, LORD, kill me instead, because I would rather die than live!" **4:4** The LORD said, "Are you really so very angry?"

4:5 Jonah left the city and sat down east of it. He made a shelter for himself there and sat down under it in the shade to see what would happen to the city. **4:6** The LORD God appointed a little plant and caused it to grow up over Jonah to be a shade over his head to rescue him from his misery. Now Jonah was very delighted about the little plant.

4:7 So God sent a worm at dawn the next day, and it attacked the little plant so that it dried up. **4:8** When the sun began to shine, God sent a hot east wind. So the sun beat down on Jonah's head, and he grew faint. So he despaired of life, and said, "I would rather die than live!" **4:9** God said to Jonah, "Are you really so very angry about the little plant?" And he said, "I am as angry as I could possibly be!" **4:10** The LORD said, "You were upset about this little plant, something for which you have not worked nor did you do anything to make it grow. It grew up overnight and died the next day. **4:11**

Should I not be even more concerned about Nineveh, this enormous city? There are more than one hundred twenty thousand people in it who do not know right from wrong, as well as many animals!"

- *You are gracious and compassionate, slow to anger and abounding in [hesed]* (4:2). Jonah knew his Hebrew catechism. He borrowed his description of God from the Lord's self-revelation in Exodus 34:6–7 to Moses on Mt. Sinai and repeated elsewhere throughout redemption history: "The Lord, the Lord, the compassionate and gracious God, slow to anger, and abounding in *[hesed]* and faithfulness, keeping *[hesed]* for thousands, forgiving iniquity and transgression and sin. But he by no means leaves the guilty unpunished, responding to the transgression of fathers by dealing with children and children's children, to the third and fourth generation.

This is the fundamental description of God that we find throughout Scripture—at least eight different times (Ex. 34:6–7; Num. 14:18; Neh. 9:17; Ps. 86:15; 103:8; 145:8; Jon. 4:2; Nah. 1:3).

2. Jonah explained his actions. Why did he say he tried to run to Tarshsish rather than accept the task God gave him (4:2)?

_____

_____

_____

3. What difference do you see between what the text says about God and anger vs. Jonah and anger (4:1, 2, 4, 9)?

_____

_____

_____

4. Many say that the God of the Old Testament is most unpleasant. Atheist Richard Dawkins in his book *The God Delusion* begins his second chapter, "The God Hypothesis," with this description of Yahweh:

"The God of the Old Testament is arguably the most unpleasant character in all fiction: jealous and proud of it; a petty, unjust, unforgiving control-freak; a vindictive, bloodthirsty ethnic cleanser; a misogynistic, homophobic, racist, infanticidal, genocidal, filicidal, pestilential, megalomaniacal, sadomasochistic, capriciously malevolent bully." Jonah, the Old Testament prophet, was a servant of Yahweh, and the prophet had in common with Dawkins that he objected to God's character. So do you think Jonah would agree with Dawkins? Why or why not?

---

5. Jonah set up a lookout outside the city to give him the best vantage point from which to see fireworks as God destroyed the oh-so-deserving Ninevites (4:5). What does this reveal about Jonah's heart?

---

6. Near the end of his ministry, Jesus sat outside a city bound for destruction too—Jerusalem. And Matthew records that Jesus said, "Jerusalem, Jerusalem, you who kill the prophets and stone those who are sent to you! How often I have longed to gather your children together as a hen gathers her chicks under her wings, but you would have none of it!" (Matt. 23:37). Contrast Jesus' and Jonah's feelings and attitudes for lost people.

Jonah's attitudes

_____

_____

_____

7. In 4:1 we find Jonah angry. But in 4:6 we see that he is "very delighted." What is the one thing that made Jonah happy in this story (4:5–6)? What does this reveal about his heart?

_____

_____

_____

_____

8. List all the times the concept of death or dying appears in today's selection from Jonah's story.

_____

_____

_____

_____

9. In Jonah 4:3, 8 we find Jonah wanting God to take his life. Why do you think Jonah felt so depressed (4:2–3)?

_____

_____

_____

10. How did God respond?

_____

_____

_____

- *Shade over his head to rescue him from his misery* (4:6). Ironically (we see the word *ironically* a lot when talking about Jonah!), the word here for "misery" is the same Hebrew word, *ra'ah*, translated earlier as "evil." God sent Jonah to pronounce judgment on the Ninevites because of their evil, and here the Lord had compassion on Jonah, rescuing him from his "evil." The plant served a dual purpose—both to shield the pouting prophet from physical discomfort and to nudge him toward a better understanding of and appreciation for God.
- *As angry as I could possibly be* (4:9). Literally, "angry to death." Jonah was suicidally mad with rage.

11. It's not unusual, actually, for a messenger of God to have a death wish following an incredibly successful experience. In 1 Kings 19:1–6 we find the account of what happens to Elijah after a huge success against false prophets:

> **1 Kings 19:1** Ahab told Jezebel all that Elijah had done, including a detailed account of how he killed all the prophets with the sword. **19:2** Jezebel sent a messenger to Elijah with this warning, "May the gods judge me severely if by this time tomorrow I do not take your life as you did theirs!" **19:3** Elijah was afraid, so he got up and fled for his life to Beer Sheba in Judah. He left his servant there, **19:4** while he went a day's journey into the desert. He went and sat down under a shrub and asked the LORD to take his life: "I've had enough! Now, O LORD, take my life. After all, I'm no better than my ancestors." **19:5** He stretched out and fell asleep under the shrub. All of a sudden an angelic messenger touched him and said, "Get up and eat." **19:6** He looked and right there by his head was a cake baking on hot coals and a jug of water. He ate and drank and then slept some more.

What similarities do you see between how God interacts with Elijah and what he does with Jonah?

_____

_____

_____

12. Moses also prayed for God to kill him. After Moses led the Israelites out of Egypt through the awesome Red Sea–parting experience, the people complained that they were better off back in Egypt. Read Numbers 11:10–17:

> **Numbers 11:10** Moses heard the people weeping throughout their families, everyone at the door of his tent; and when the anger of the Lord was kindled greatly, Moses was also displeased. **11:11** And Moses said to the LORD, "Why have you afflicted your servant? Why have I not found favor in your sight, that you lay the burden of this entire people on me? **11:12** Did I conceive this entire people? Did I give birth to them, that you should say to me, 'Carry them in your arms, as a foster father bears a nursing child,' to the land which you swore to their fathers? **11:13** From where shall I get meat to give to this entire people, for they cry to me, 'Give us meat, that we may eat!' **11:14** I am not able to bear this entire people alone, because it is too heavy for me! **11:15** But if you are going to deal with me like this, then kill me immediately. If I have found favor in your sight then do not let me see my trouble." **11:16** The LORD said to Moses, "Gather to me seventy men of the elders of Israel, whom you know are elders of the people and officials over them, and bring them to the tent of meeting; let them take their position there with you. **11:17** Then I will come down and speak with you there, and I will take part of the spirit that is on you, and will put it on them, and they will bear some of the burden of the people with you, so that you do not bear it all by yourself.

What was the cause of Moses' depression, and how did God respond?

_____

_____

_____

_____

2. How were Elijah and Moses similar to Jonah? How did they differ?

_____

_____

_____

3. What do all these Bible stories reveal to us about God?

_____

_____

_____

- *More than one hundred twenty thousand people in it who do not know right from wrong* (4:11). The Hebrew literally says that the people do not know "their right hand from their left." Many have taken this to mean that the city had more than one hundred twenty thousand infants and toddlers who weren't even old enough to know the difference. Yet it's more likely that God was speaking here of moral ignorance. The people (*'adam*), while accountable for their great evil, had not had the access to the Word and prophets of God available to Israel. Touché. Here Jonah was so obsessed with justice, and the judge of all the world silenced him by helping him see his unjust assessment.

THURSDAY: AN OBJECT LESSON

1. Pray for insight; then read the ending to Jonah's tale:

> **Jonah 4:7** So God sent a worm at dawn the next day, and it attacked the little plant so that it dried up. **4:8** When the sun began to shine, God sent a hot east wind. So the sun beat down on Jonah's

head, and he grew faint. So he despaired of life, and said, "I would rather die than live!" **4:9** God said to Jonah, "Are you really so very angry about the little plant?" And he said, "I am as angry as I could possibly be!" **4:10** The LORD said, "You were upset about this little plant, something for which you have not worked nor did you do anything to make it grow. It grew up overnight and died the next day. **4:11** Should I not be even more concerned about Nineveh, this enormous city? There are more than one hundred twenty thousand people in it who do not know right from wrong, as well as many animals!"

2. What was the source of the worm (4:7)? Was God trying to punish Jonah? Explain your answer.

_____

_____

_____

3. Jonah was far more concerned about shade and comfort than about the destinies of Nineveh's citizens. What are some ways in which we find ourselves so engrossed in creature comforts that we lose sight of the lost souls around us? (Do we spend more time concerned with our pets than with lost people? Do we get more upset about sunburns than about the eternal destiny awaiting unbelievers?)

_____

_____

_____

4. Pray, asking for wisdom; then consider some ways you can rearrange your priorities to put first things first. What comes to mind?

_____

_____

_____

5. Why do you think God didn't just let the Book of Jonah end at chapter 3? After all, mission accomplished, right?

_____

_____

_____

_____

6. God used three visual aids to teach Jonah—a little plant, a worm, and a hot east wind. How did he use each (4:6–8)? What was God attempting to teach Jonah with each?

Little plant

_____

_____

_____

Worm

_____

_____

_____

Hot east wind

_____

_____

_____

_____

7. Do you ever get upset because God shows grace to someone you don't think deserves it?

_____

_____

_____

8. Do you ever, like Jonah, long for God to destroy someone rather than to show mercy? What about a woman who murders her children, a serial killer, a child-mutilating rapist, murderous religious extremists, or—more specifically—Saddam Hussein (a Ninevite from recent history). Explain your answer.

_____

_____

_____

9. Back in 1999 a missionary in Colombia, South America, wrote:

We would appreciate your prayers for us especially in the area of coping with the day-to-day stress of living here. The situation politically has deteriorated rapidly this fall and has caused great concern among the missionary community. To speak frankly, at times we are just hanging in there. The frustrations we run into culturally are at times more intense as the war for this nation's survival progresses. I daily have to remind myself that I don't have to love these people because frankly it's impossible at times! But

We read in 2 Peter 3:7 the description of a coming day when God will punish those who commit evil. Five verses later Peter speaks positively of his readers looking forward to that day. So the desire for ultimate justice is a godly desire. But Jesus tells us to love our enemies (Luke 6:27, 35). Our desire and prayer should be that the wicked repent and that God will extend mercy to them when they do. But if they don't, we are not expected to desire that the unrepentant will go unpunished. To desire ultimate justice is to desire what God also desires.

God loves them and died for them and I only have to be His open channel through which His love can flow. Pray for me not to be a 'Jonah' and resent being used.

Do you face situations in which God is using you but you're struggling to love people who need the Lord?

_____

_____

_____

10. What are some actions that might indicate an attitude of superiority, prejudice, or bigotry toward others whom God has created?

_____

_____

_____

My friend Dorian, a Hebrew scholar, wrote this about the last chapter of Jonah:

I am impressed by the drama of chapter 4. Imagine a teenager in the kitchen. He is standing there wearing the underwear and socks and the shirt and jeans that one of his parents recently took out of the dryer for him and having just eaten the breakfast that they provided. He is complaining. His mom or dad asks him a polite question, and he stalks off without replying. How would that have gone over in the home in which you grew up? Jonah does this, having been rescued from certain death and having bragged about his superiority to the pagans. God is putting up with a lot and still attempting to persuade Jonah to change his mind. The book offers several opportunities for comparisons between Jonah and the people around him, and they all behave better than he does. But in the end it is God's own character and actions with which he must compare himself.

I don't, by the way, think that God was telling Jonah that there was an "ought" about what He did for the people of Nineveh. God wasn't saying that He was morally obligated to let the Ninevites off because they had repented. For the sake of argument, He accepted Jonah's right to be concerned about the plant. ("If it is okay for you to care about the plant, wouldn't it be okay for me to care about these people?")

11. **Bonus Question:** Christian art in the early centuries focused a lot on the Jonah story. Do a Web search and see if you can find examples. Then create your own visual piece based on the story, or make jewelry or write a poem.

FRIDAY: THE WHOLE PICTURE

1. Time to put it all together. Pray for God to reveal to you attitudes that need to change as you reread the Book of Jonah focusing on Jonah's desire for judgment vs. God's desire to relent.

Jonah 1

1:1 The LORD said to Jonah son of Amittai, 1:2 "Go immediately to Nineveh, that large capital city, and announce judgment against its people because their wickedness has come to my attention." 1:3 Instead, Jonah immediately headed off to Tarshish to escape from the commission of the LORD. He traveled to Joppa and found a merchant ship heading to Tarshish. So he paid the fare and went aboard it to go with them to Tarshish far away from the LORD. 1:4 But the LORD hurled a powerful wind on the sea. Such a violent tempest arose on the sea that the ship threatened to break up! 1:5 The sailors were so afraid that each cried out to his own god and they flung the ship's cargo overboard to make the ship lighter. Jonah, meanwhile, had gone down into the hold below deck, had lain down, and was sound asleep. 1:6 The ship's captain approached him and said, "What are you doing asleep? Get up! Cry out to your god! Perhaps your god might take notice of us so that we might not die!" 1:7 The sailors said to one another, "Come on, let's cast lots to find out whose fault it is that this disaster has overtaken us." So they cast lots, and Jonah was singled out. 1:8 They said to him, "Tell us, whose fault is it that this disaster has overtaken us? What's your occupation? Where do you come from? What's your country? And who are your people?" **1:9** He said to them, "I am a Hebrew! And I worship the LORD, the God of heaven, who made the sea and the dry land." **1:10** Hearing this, the men became even more afraid and said to him, "What have you done?" (The men said this because they knew that he was trying to escape from the LORD, because he had previously told them.) **1:11** Because the storm was growing worse and worse, they said to him, "What should we do to you to make the sea calm down for us?" **1:12** He said to them, "Pick me up and throw me into the sea to make the sea quiet down, because I know it's my fault you are in this severe storm." **1:13** Instead, they tried to row back to land, but they were not able to do so because the storm kept growing worse and worse. **1:14** So they cried out to the LORD, "Oh, please, LORD, don't let us die on account of this man! Don't hold us guilty of shedding innocent blood. After all, you, LORD, have done just as you pleased." **1:15** So they picked Jonah up and threw him into the sea, and the sea stopped raging. **1:16** The men feared the LORD greatly, and earnestly vowed to offer lavish sacrifices to the LORD.

1:17 The LORD sent a huge fish to swallow Jonah, and Jonah was in the stomach of the fish three days and three nights.

Jonah 2

2:1 Jonah prayed to the LORD his God from the stomach of the fish

2:2 and said, "I called out to the LORD from my distress,
and he answered me;
from the belly of Sheol I cried out for help,
and you heard my prayer.
2:3 You threw me into the deep waters,
into the middle of the sea;
the ocean current engulfed me;
all the mighty waves you sent swept over me.
2:4 I thought I had been banished from your sight,
that I would never again see your holy temple!
2:5 Water engulfed me up to my neck;
the deep ocean surrounded me;
seaweed was wrapped around my head.

2:6 I went down to the very bottoms of the mountains;

the gates of the netherworld barred me in forever;

but you brought me up from the Pit, O LORD , my God.

2:7 When my life was ebbing away, I called out to the LORD,

and my prayer came to your holy temple.

2:8 Those who worship worthless idols forfeit the mercy that could be theirs.

2:9 But as for me, I promise to offer a sacrifice to you with a public declaration of praise;

I will surely do what I have promised.

Salvation belongs to the LORD!"

2:10 Then the LORD commanded the fish and it disgorged Jonah on dry land.

Jonah 3

3:1 The LORD said to Jonah a second time, **3:2** "Go immediately to Nineveh, that large city, and proclaim to it the message that I tell you." **3:3** So Jonah went immediately to Nineveh, as the LORD had said. (Now Nineveh was an enormous city—it required three days to walk through it!) **3:4** When Jonah began to enter the city one day's walk, he announced, "At the end of forty days, Nineveh will be overthrown!"

3:5 The people of Nineveh believed in God, and they declared a fast and put on sackcloth, from the greatest to the least of them. **3:6** When the news reached the king of Nineveh, he got up from his throne, took off his royal robe, put on sackcloth, and sat on ashes. **3:7** He issued a proclamation and said, "In Nineveh, by the decree of the king and his nobles: No human or animal, cattle or sheep, is to taste anything; they must not eat and they must not drink water. **3:8** Every person and animal must put on sackcloth and must cry earnestly to God, and everyone must turn from their evil way of living and from the violence that they do. **3:9** Who knows? Perhaps God might be willing to change his mind and relent and turn from his fierce anger so that we might not die." **3:10** When God saw their actions—they turned from their evil way of living!—God relented concerning the judgment he had threatened them with and he did not destroy them.

Jonah 4

4:1 This displeased Jonah terribly and he became very angry. **4:2** He prayed to the LORD and said, "Oh, LORD, this is just what I thought would happen when I was in my own country. This is what I tried to prevent by attempting to escape to Tarshish!—because I knew that you are gracious and compassionate, slow to anger and abounding in mercy, and one who relents concerning threatened judgment. **4:3** So now, LORD, kill me instead, because I would rather die than live!" **4:4** The LORD said, "Are you really so very angry?"

4:5 Jonah left the city and sat down east of it. He made a shelter for himself there and sat down under it in the shade to see what would happen to the city. **4:6** The LORD God appointed a little plant and caused it to grow up over Jonah to be a shade over his head to rescue him from his misery. Now Jonah was very delighted about the little plant.

4:7 So God sent a worm at dawn the next day, and it attacked the little plant so that it dried up. **4:8** When the sun began to shine, God sent a hot east wind. So the sun beat down on Jonah's head, and he grew faint. So he despaired of life, and said, "I would rather die than live!" **4:9** God said to Jonah, "Are you really so very angry about the little plant?" And he said, "I am as angry as I could possibly be!" **4:10** The LORD said, "You were upset about this little plant, something for which you have not worked nor did you do anything to make it grow. It grew up overnight and died the next day. **4:11** Should I not be even more concerned about Nineveh, this enormous city? There are more than one hundred twenty thousand people in it who do not know right from wrong, as well as many animals!"

2. What elements in the story stood out to you as you spent the past month exploring this book of the Bible?

_____

_____

_____

_____

2. Look back through your notes. What in your life needs to change in response to what you have learned? What conversations do you still need to have? What actions do you need to pursue?

_____

_____

_____

3. Write out your remaining plan of action below. Pray through your decisions. Ask for guidance and strength.

_____

_____

_____

4. List here people who need to know about the love of God and his desire to relent concerning judgment. Pray about having conversations with them.

_____

_____

_____

5. Select a people group that still has not heard or responded to the gospel. Spend some time praying for them.

SATURDAY: BE RECONCILED!

My friend Dorian, whom I mentioned earlier, teaches seminary Hebrew classes. The opening chapters of Jonah make for relatively easy translation, as translations go. So she has spent a lot of time in those chapters, walking her students through them. And she makes some interesting observations about the dynamics between Jonah and

God. She has noticed that when people pose the question, Does God change his mind? they tend to get tied up in philosophical or theological questions about the nature of God. Yet she thinks a closer reading of the text may be in order. "When God announces impending judgment," she says, "we need to observe whether or not He also has sworn an oath that confirms that the matter of judgment is settled." Apparently when God has not sworn an oath, the threat may be either a warning *or* a decree. Of course, the hearers don't know which until they repent and see if God spares them from the consequences of their actions. At the heart of the matter, Dorian says, is "whether God takes humans seriously or views us as harmless little pets." She writes:

> We tend to think that He owes us because we are so cute and loveable. But if the opposite is the case, He does not owe anyone a warning about impending judgment. Any announcement of impending judgment is an implied opportunity to repent, which is simply the right response. We should agree with God, whether or not He will stop the impending calamity. Jonah knows from the history of Israel (not to mention his recent experience), that the Lord is just the sort who tends to relent when people repent—and sometimes even when they don't.
>
> The Lord and Jonah are having this conversation because the Lord did not destroy Jonah in the Mediterranean or Jonah's gene pool back in Exodus 32–34 [which we read last week]. Jonah knows all the right words about God and knows how He operates, but Jonah doesn't like Him. Chapter 4 shows us that God wants to persuade Jonah to agree with Him, not just do what He says. If the issue were merely about getting Jonah to do as he's told or if it were about getting a message to the Ninevites, the book could have ended with chapter 3. In chapter 4, God is doing for Jonah what Paul does for the Christians at Corinth when he begs them, "Be reconciled to God!"

Have you been reconciled to God? Have you trusted in the work of Christ to bear the consequences you deserve for your sins?

Or are you—like Jonah—happy to receive grace but not so excited when God grants it to others? Do you pray for enemy soldiers to know him? Do you pray for people you can hardly stand to come to faith?

Do you look down on other nations or races or people groups as being inferior to yours? What about those in different socioeconomic groups? Do you despise the rich? Think you're better than the poor? Loathe AIDS patients? Act rudely to those who support gay marriage and abortion? Lose patience quickly with those far more conservative than you?

Do you rejoice when people less deserving than you have cause for rejoicing? Or does grace make you angry?

If not, have you "gotten over" grace? Or does its sweet sound still thrill you every day God gives you breath?

The Book of Jonah has shown us that God is everywhere and that his love has no limits—even to the point of seeming excessive. He wants us both to obey *and* to trust. Will you trust his heart?

"God so loved the world . . ." and he wants to use you as a messenger. Will you, like Jonah, run the other way? Or will you obey by going and speaking for him? The task may seem a little scary at times, but you are never, ever alone.

Pray: *Heavenly Father, thank you for grace—your grace to the nations, and your grace to my country, and your grace to the body of Christ worldwide, and your grace to me! Make me a blessing, a channel of grace to the undeserving. Help me never get over the unmerited favor I've received from you. I confess my pride and repent. Help me to have a humble heart toward you. Make me the kind of person to whom you enjoy giving ever more abundant measures of grace. Give me a heart of hesed, that when people see my attitudes and my actions, they see something of my wonderful Father reflected in my eyes. In the name of your Son, amen.*

Memorize: "In Christ God was reconciling the world to himself, not counting people's trespasses against them, and he has given us the message of reconciliation. Therefore we are ambassadors for Christ, as though God were making His plea through us. We plead with you on Christ's behalf, 'Be reconciled to God!' God made the one who did not know sin to be sin for us, so that in him we would become the righteousness of God" (2 Cor. 5:19–21).

LEADER'S GUIDE

To direct a Coffee Cup Bible study, you do not need to have a seminary degree, be a public speaker, or even possess the spiritual gift of teaching. You need only to have a desire to see people grow through God's Word and a genuine concern for their spiritual growth. Often the person best suited to the facilitator's role is not someone who likes to impart knowledge (teaching). Rather, it's someone who enjoys drawing out others and hearing *them* talk (encouragement). Pray, asking the Lord to guide you. Do you sense God leading you to facilitate a group?

Getting Started

Pray about whom you should invite to join you. Then begin inviting participants and set a deadline for commitments. Ask yourself the best way to communicate to others the opportunity for group study—church bulletin? Web site? blog? text? e-mail? flier? poster? phone call?

If you envision a church-sponsored study with a number of small groups, aim to give participants at least several months' notice so you can schedule a room and so participants can add the event to their calendars. Work with the appropriate church servants to work out details relating to time and place.

If you plan to gather a small group of friends, decide as a group the best time and place to meet. Ideally, small groups should be no larger than eight to ten members.

Take book orders, collect payment, and distribute books in advance or have each individual take care of obtaining her own. The former is recommended, however, as bulk discounts are often available, and people are more likely to follow through in attending if they have a study in hand.

Pray for each person who will be attending, asking that God's presence would be known and that each would have a desire to learn the Word.

KICK OFF

Before your first Bible discussion time, hold a kick-off brunch or get your group together at church, a coffee shop, or in a home. Open with prayer.

Provide opportunities for members to get acquainted if they don't already know each other. Do this by providing introductions or offering some icebreaker questions that include each participant giving her name and some background information. You might ask a benign question with the potential for humor, such as What is your favorite household appliance? Encourage them to think creatively beyond the refrigerator—what about the water heater? Blender? Coffee maker? Their answers can reveal a lot about them. And this will help people open up to each other. One artist-led group asked this question and provided Play-Doh so each participant could make an image of her appliance of choice, and others had to guess what it was.

You will need to determine before this meeting whether to distribute studies in advance or to hand them out at this event. You will also need to decide if members should read only the introduction the first week or if they are to read both the introduction and complete the first week of study. (If the former, plan for how you will fill the time at your first meeting, as you will have little to discuss. Perhaps you can do a service project together, such as writing to a child whom a group member sponsors. Or share your own faith story so your group can get to know you.)

Something else you'll need to determine—do you want to complete each chapter in one week, or do you want to spread your study out over an eight-week period? If the latter, determine where to divide the questions for each week's study.

Obtain permission to distribute contact information among the members to encourage discussion and fellowship throughout the week. Include phone, e-mail, and social networking and street address information.

YOUR FIRST DISCUSSION MEETING

When the group gathers for the first discussion, be sure all participants meet each other if they haven't already. Distribute contact information, and be sure everyone has a study handy.

You will spend most of your time in discussion. If your group members hardly know each other or seem reluctant to talk, use an icebreaker question to get them started. Try to come up with something that relates to the topic without requiring a spiritual answer. You may have people in your group who are completely uncomfortable talking about spiritual things, and the icebreaker is a less-threatening way to help them participate. In fact, for these reasons you might want to include an icebreaker at the beginning of each discussion to get lighthearted conversation going. See the list of suggestions in the next section.

YOUR WEEKLY MEETING

Begin each session with prayer and do your best to start on time, depending on the formality of the group. Set a clear ending time and respect participants' schedules.

After prayer, ask the icebreaker question, if you plan to use one. Then move to discussion. Plan to allow about forty-five minutes for this time. Select the questions you'll ask by going back through the lesson for the week and choosing about seven open-ended questions. You can simply circle in your guide the questions you want to ask. Be sure at least one of your choices covers what you feel is the most important point from the text for that week.

Be careful not to dominate as the leader. Your job is not to instruct but to draw out. If you have a member who rarely says anything, periodically direct an easy question specifically to her.

When you finish the final question, ask members if they want to share prayer requests, items for thanksgiving, or announcements. Be sure each prayer request is actually prayed over, and encourage the group to refrain from answering such requests with advice or related stories ("I know someone else with that kind of cancer and she used a herbal supplement . . .").

When you're finished, be sure each person knows the next assignment and the meeting time and place for your next study.

Between meetings, pray for participants. It will mean a lot if you can follow up with a phone call, particularly when people have shared urgent requests.

ICEBREAKERS

Week 1. The text for week 1 focuses on Jonah heading for an exotic locale rather than a doomed city. So you could ask, "What place would you most like to visit and why?" The text also includes Jonah thrown overboard with the prospect of drowning. So if members already know each other well, you could ask a more intense question, such as, "How would you most or least like to die?"

Week 2. The text for week 2 is Jonah's prayer in the belly of the fish. You could ask members to describe the scariest situation they've ever faced or the most desperate situation they've ever been in. Or, because Jonah pulls together words from a smattering of known phrases in the psalms, you could ask your group to fill in the rest of a popular phrase from which you've deleted some words. Choose from these or come up with your own:

"When it absolutely positively has to be there overnight."
"All the news that's fit to print."
"Silent night, holy night, all is calm, all is bright."
"Roses are red, violets are blue."
"Let your fingers do the walking through the Yellow Pages."

Week 3. The subject for week 3 is confession and repentance. You could begin with a question such as, "Share a time when you were given a second chance or when you gave someone else a second chance." If the group seems comfortable being vulnerable, ask, "What's one of the dumbest things you've ever done?" You as the leader will set the stage for how open members are with their faults. If you go first and share your foibles, they will be more inclined to do likewise.

Because writing their testimony is part of each person's assignment for week 3, this may be a good time to lead off with your own testimony. Again, the more open you are about your flaws, the more you will set the stage for honest sharing from the group.

When participants do share their testimonies, be sure the group affirms each one verbally in some way rather than sitting in stony silence afterward.

Week 4. In Jonah 4 we find God asking the prophet a number of questions rather than making statements. So you could ask the group, "What question would you like someone to ask you and how would you answer?" or "What is one of the most interesting questions anyone has ever asked you and how did you answer?" A more intense possibility that relates to the subject matter for the week is, "What evidences of bigotry and prejudice do you see in and outside of the church today?"

More than Bible Study

Perhaps you would like to combine your time in Bible study with service. You can choose from the following ways to do so or come up with your own ideas.

Have each person bring something every week to donate. One week, they can bring used eye glasses. The next it's cell phones to recycle; then used Bibles to go to an organization that distributes them to the needy or in countries where Bibles are not readily available. Finally, donate books to the public library or your church library.

Other possibilities are combining your time with a baby shower to benefit a Pregnancy Resource Center or assembling Christmas boxes for Samaritan's Purse. You can involve the group in deciding what they want to do.

Combine your study with your church's missionary needs. One week have everyone bring supplies for someone's mission trip, such as power bars, dried soup, and seeds. Often short-term teams need items such as translators' gifts and VBS prizes. My congregation's sister-church in Mexico sometimes asks for school supplies in September. Missionaries in Mexico ask for Spanish Bibles. You could ask your congregation's Webmaster to set up an Amazon Associates' account with a link through your church's Web pages; then direct all members to order through the link. Choose a mission to benefit from all proceeds. Yet another possibility is bringing office and bathroom supplies for your church.

Target a people group to learn about and pray for as part of your time together.

Adopt a missionary of the week or month to pray for and to learn about each time you meet.

Choose a group within your community to serve. If a nursing home, volunteer together one week. If the local homeless shelter, donate pillowcases, or learn to knit and send scarves in the winter. If your local firefighters need your support, take cookies. Volunteer to pick up trash in an area where your city has a need.

By linking time in God's Word with time serving others, you will help group members move from compartmentalizing to integrating their discipleship time and the stewardship of their resources.

Lists of and links to additional helps for your Bible discussion time are available at www.aspire2.com in the Coffee Cup Bible Study section of the site. If your group generates ideas they want to share with others, send them through the contact page on the aspire2 Web site. We'd love to know what ideas worked for you!

Perhaps you have some artists in your group who need more right-brained interaction. Encourage them to create songs, jewelry, paintings, photos, collages, poetry, prayers, psalms—the options for creative interaction in response to the truths learned in Jonah are endless. Remember that examples of others' creations made in conjunction with Bible study are available in the galleries at www.soulpersuit.com.

God bless you as you serve the body of Christ in this way!

Other Books in the Coffee Cup Bible Study Series®

Espresso with Esther
Java with the Judges
Mocha on the Mount
Solomon Latte
Premium Roast with Ruth
Cappuccino with Colossians
Frappé with Philippians

About the NET BIBLE®

The NET BIBLE® is an exciting new translation of the Bible with 60,932 translators' notes! These translators' notes make the original Greek, Hebrew and Aramaic texts of the Bible far more accessible and unlocks the riches of the Bible's truth from entirely new perspectives.

The NET BIBLE® is the first modern Bible to be completely free for anyone, anywhere in the world to download as part of a powerful new "Ministry First" approach being pioneered at bible.org.

**Download the entire NET Bible and
60,932 notes for free at www.bible.org**

About the bible.org ministry

Before there was eBay® . . . before there was Amazon.com® . . . there was bible.org! Bible.org is a non-profit (501c3) Christian ministry headquartered in Dallas, Texas. In the last decade bible.org has grown to serve millions of individuals around the world and provides thousands of trustworthy resources for Bible study (2 Tim 2:2).

**Go to www.bible.org for thousands
of trustworthy resources including:**

- The NET BIBLE®
- Discipleship Materials
- The Theology Program
- More than 10,000 Sermon Illustrations
- ABC's of Christian Growth
- Bible Dictionaries and Commentaries